BBC ACTIVE

BUSINESS STUDIES

Complete Revision Guide

Paul Clark

Published by BBC Active, an imprint of Educational Publishers LLP, part of the Pearson Education Group
Edinburgh Gate, Harlow, Essex CN20 2JE, England

ISBN: 978-1-4066-1374-2

Printed in China GCC/01

The Publisher's policy is to use paper manufactured from sustainable forests.

First published 2002
This edition 2007

Contents

About Bitesize

GCSE Bitesize is a revision service designed to help you achieve success at GCSE. There are books, television programmes and a website, each of which provides a separate resource designed to help you get the best results.

TV programmes are available on video through your school or you can find out transmission times by calling **08700 100 222.**

The website can be found at http://www.bbc.co.uk/schools/gcsebitesize/

About this book

This book is your all-in-one revision companion for GCSE.
It gives you the three things you need for successful revision:

1. Every topic clearly organised and clearly explained.

2. The most important facts and ideas highlighted for quick checking: in each topic and in the extra sections at the end of this book.

3. All the practice you need: in the 'check' questions in the margins, in the practice sections at the end of each topic, and in the exam questions section at the end of this book.

Each topic is organised in the same way:

- **The Bare Bones** – a summary of the main points, an introduction to the topic, and a good way to check what you know.

- **Key facts** highlighted throughout.

- **Check questions** in the margin at the end of each section of the topic - have you understood this bit?

- **Remember tips** in the margin – extra advice on this section of the topic.

- **Exam tips in red** – specific things to bear in mind for the exam.

- **Practice questions** at the end of each topic to check your understanding.

The extra sections at the back of this book will help you check your progress and be confident that you know your stuff:

- **Exam questions and model answers:** a selection of exam questions with the model answers explained to help you get full marks plus extra questions for you to complete (answers in the answer section).

- **Topic checker:** quick questions in all topic areas. As you revise a set of topics, see if you can answer these questions – put ticks or crosses next to them.

About this book *continued*

The next time you revise those topics, try the questions again. Do this until you've got a column of ticks.

- **Complete the facts:** another resource for you to use as you revise – fill in the gaps to complete the facts (answers in the answer section).
- **Last-minute learner:** the most important facts in just four pages.

GCSE Business studies exam questions

GCSE Business studies students are entered at one of two levels - Foundation or Higher Tier. There are examples of questions from both levels in this book. The questions vary from course to course, but most papers have some **short questions**, on particular topics, which require answers of one or two sentences or paragraphs (it will be clear from the style of question, and the space allowed in the answer booklet, how long your answer should be). Other questions are based on **case studies**, with source material to study. (This material, in some cases, is supplied before the exam.) These questions test your knowledge and understanding from right across the course, not just from one topic.

Case study questions are generally in two or three parts and the source material may include such things as photographs, drawings, newspaper cuttings, company information, tables or graphs. Typical first questions will ask about your understanding of this data, for example, 'What do you understand by the term...'. Foundation Tier papers will normally just have two or three of this type of question.

Higher Tier papers generally have more extended case studies and problem-solving exercises, and questions are often 'open-ended', which means that there could be a range of possible answers. You are asked to evaluate or suggest solutions to business problems, and should list the points and data you would use to support your ideas. Typical questions include 'Why do you think the business chose to...', 'Explain the effect that this decision will have on...' and 'How can the firm improve its sales figures...'. There is usually more than one viewpoint on any problem. Make it clear, for example, if you are writing as a manager, a worker or a customer.

Use examples from real businesses wherever possible to support your explanations.

Understanding the questions

GCSE exams are not trying to catch you out. They aim to give you the opportunity to show what you know, in a clear, well-constructed way. So it's important that you read each question carefully and make sure you understand what it is asking you to do. Below are some words commonly used in business studies exam questions. Make sure you understand exactly what they mean.

Compare - identify and write down the similarities and differences between features stated in the question.

Define - write a definition of, describe accurately or explain the meaning of.

Describe - write down details about what is shown in a resource such as a bar chart, newspaper report or graph.

Discuss (or **Analyse**) - usually requires a longer answer examining, describing and giving reasons. Also, maybe, explaining arguments for and against.

Explain (or **Account for**) - give reasons for a business decision or activity.

Give your views - say what you think or what another individual or group of people might think.

Identify - name, recognise or select a particular feature or features.

Name, state or **list** - write key points (detailed explanations are not required).

Study - look carefully at a resource and think about what it shows.

With reference to (or **refer to**) **examples that you have studied** - when explaining the reasons for a particular answer, include details of specific case studies or other examples.

With the help of (or **using**) **the information provided** - include examples from the information on the exam paper to explain your answer.

Planning your revision

The secret of good revision is planning. Prepare a revision timetable three or four months before your exams, with time allotted to each of your subjects. Divide the days by the number of subjects, so you know how much time you've got for each. Then organize the time into batches - about three 40-minute sessions per day is enough for most people, and it is a good idea to keep to one subject per day. Each subject should have some early batches of time allocated to basic learning and understanding, then some later sessions for self-testing and practice in answering questions.

Make sure your timetable includes short breaks between the sessions, and longer time-off slots, e.g. for sport or leisure. If you revise too hard for too long, you will not remember things very well.

What to revise

Your main revision aims should be to improve your **knowledge** and understanding of business ideas and behaviour, to improve your **recall** (your ability to 'unlock' this knowledge when it is needed) and also to learn how to **adapt** what you know, so that you can **apply** it to answering a wide range of questions. Below is a checklist to work from when going through your revision material. It will improve your level of marks in the exam if you have these basic elements covered:

- key business terms

- examples of good business case studies

- information about, and explanations of, business decisions and behaviour

- causes and effects, e.g. impacts of technology or price changes on a business

- similarities and differences between business organisations

- attitudes and values of different interest groups

- alternative views

- advantages and disadvantages of different solutions to issues

How to revise

Organise the information you are trying to learn into short notes, lists, sketches, diagrams, flow charts, codes and tables. This will help you to learn it and makes it easier to **memorise**. Try to bring together all your information from different sources in this way. Memorising should always be based on: **look, cover, write, check**. As you go through this book, try working in this way. Close the book after reading each double page and write down the key facts it covered.

To revise well, you should read through your notes and lists on a regular basis, test your memory by checking and rechecking and, importantly, practise answering questions of different kinds. It is a good idea to get hold of some old exam papers - your teacher should be able to help you with this. You'll find that the same kind of question comes up year after year, so you can see the type of thing to expect.

On the day

At the start of the exam, remember to read and follow all the instructions on the front of each paper. If there is a choice of questions, read through each one carefully to make sure you choose the one(s) you know the most about. It is a good idea to quickly plan out the longer answers, writing brief notes to remind yourself what to include.

Assess the time allowed overall, and the different lengths of the questions, to work out how much time to give each. Some exam papers may say how many marks each question is worth, which gives you a clue as to how detailed each answer should be and how long you should spend on it. Check your time during the exam and don't spend too long on one question. If you haven't left enough time to answer a question properly, write down all your thoughts in an organised list of notes, to show the examiners how you would have approached the question. This will get you some marks.

Write neatly and clearly and check your spelling, punctuation and grammar. Examiners cannot award marks to something they cannot read, and extra marks may be given for good English, particularly the correct spelling of specialist terms.

Business types & objectives

THE BARE BONES

Businesses can be classified (grouped together) in different ways:
- ➤ by sectors of activity or industrial groupings
- ➤ by the way they are financed and controlled
- ➤ by their different objectives.

A Different types of business

Business types include sole traders, partnerships, companies and co-operatives.

KEY FACT

Different business types can be linked together in a chain of production.

Remember
There are usually many types of business within an industry. Bigger businesses are more likely to be companies.

Q What is a chain of production?

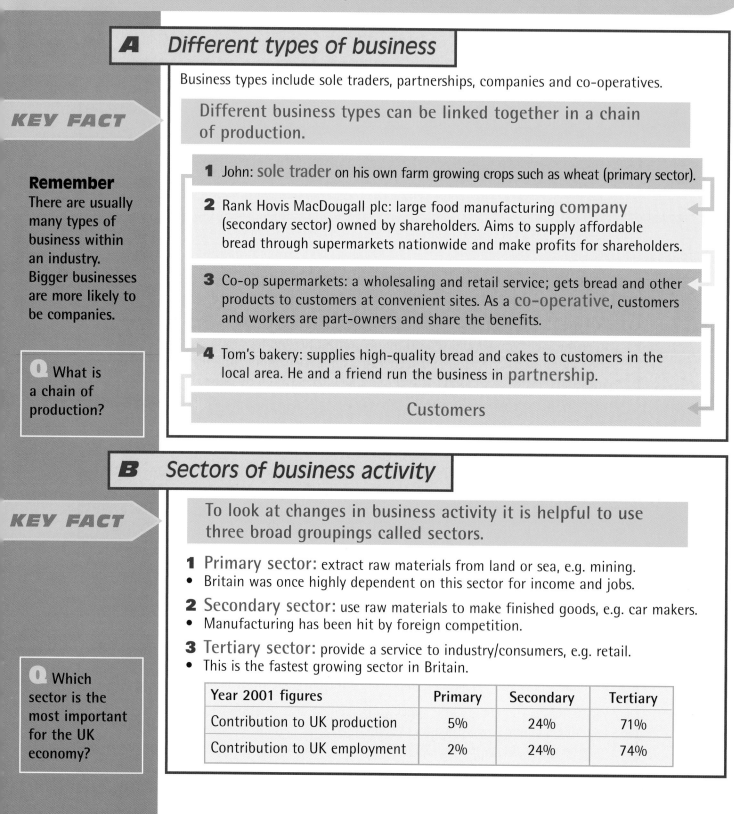

1 John: sole trader on his own farm growing crops such as wheat (primary sector).

2 Rank Hovis MacDougall plc: large food manufacturing company (secondary sector) owned by shareholders. Aims to supply affordable bread through supermarkets nationwide and make profits for shareholders.

3 Co-op supermarkets: a wholesaling and retail service; gets bread and other products to customers at convenient sites. As a co-operative, customers and workers are part-owners and share the benefits.

4 Tom's bakery: supplies high-quality bread and cakes to customers in the local area. He and a friend run the business in partnership.

Customers

B Sectors of business activity

KEY FACT

To look at changes in business activity it is helpful to use three broad groupings called sectors.

1 Primary sector: extract raw materials from land or sea, e.g. mining.
- Britain was once highly dependent on this sector for income and jobs.

2 Secondary sector: use raw materials to make finished goods, e.g. car makers.
- Manufacturing has been hit by foreign competition.

3 Tertiary sector: provide a service to industry/consumers, e.g. retail.
- This is the fastest growing sector in Britain.

Q Which sector is the most important for the UK economy?

Year 2001 figures	Primary	Secondary	Tertiary
Contribution to UK production	5%	24%	71%
Contribution to UK employment	2%	24%	74%

C Chain of production

Businesses in one sector are linked to, and dependent on, those in other sectors. At each stage in the chain a business will try to add value.

A chain of production for the oil industry (as shown here) and for the bread industry (opposite) demonstrates the interdependence of businesses.

Q Describe the chain of production for a garden shed.

Oil extraction (primary) → Oil refining (secondary) – produces a range of products, e.g. petrol, plastics → Retail (tertiary), e.g. petrol stations

D Business integration

Businesses may link their production activities across different sectors. This is called <u>integration</u>.

Remember
A business can expand by taking over/merging with a competing business or one at a different stage in the production chain.

1 Vertical integration: a business links with another in a different sector:

- **Backward integration:** a business links backwards in the chain of production. Example: an oil refining company becomes involved with extraction.
- **Forward integration:** a business links forwards in the chain of production. Example: an oil refining company takes over a group of petrol stations.

2 Horizontal integration: a business links with another in the same sector. Example: two oil refineries merge.

E Industry groupings

Business activities can be classified into eight industrial groupings.

Q In which group would you find supermarkets?

1 The groupings are: agriculture, forestry, fishing; distribution, hotels, repairs; energy and water; transport and communication; manufacturing; construction; banking, finance, insurance; education and health.

2 They can be used to examine changes in employment and production, and are widely used in government statistics.

PRACTICE

1 Classify each of the following businesses as either primary, secondary or tertiary:
   a) a food manufacturer   b) a fishing company
   c) a car repair centre   d) a private school

2 What kind of integration is represented by:
   a) a car manufacturer taking over a car dealer?
   b) a jeweller's shop merging with a craft store?

Different types of business

THE BARE BONES

➤ Businesses can be classified by how they are owned and financed, and on the basis of their legal responsibilities.

➤ A sole trader is a business owned and controlled by one person. Partnerships are owned by at least two partners.

A Sole traders and partnerships

KEY FACT

1 Sole traders (sole proprietors) and partnerships are the <u>smallest</u> forms of business but are the easiest to set up.

- They make an important contribution to the economy, accounting for over 90% of UK businesses.

- They carry big risks of failure and of incurring debts for their owners, but they also allow individuals to turn an enterprising idea or skill into a business activity.

KEY FACT

2 A sole trader is a business owned and controlled by one person.

- Sole traders operate under their own name and assume responsibility for the running of the business. They are the most common type of business in the UK.

KEY FACT

3 Partnerships are owned by the partners. There must be a minimum of two and usually a maximum of twenty partners.

- Responsibilities can be shared, with the business benefiting from the expertise of all the partners.

- There is less disruption when someone leaves the business as other partners remain to share their knowledge and keep contact with customers.

- Most partnerships write a Deed of Partnership – a set of rules to follow if trust between partners breaks down. A Deed usually **covers the sharing of profits and losses**, the <u>financial contribution</u> of each partner, their **responsibilities, and how partners may be added to or removed from the business.** Under the 1980 Partnership Act, everything is shared equally if there is no Deed or similar formal agreement.

Remember
Partnerships are common in professions like medicine and law where businesses are not allowed to limit their liability.

Q Define the terms sole trader and partnership.

1 Have unlimited liability, which means the owners are personally responsible for the debts of the business.

Sole traders and partnerships

3 Finance comes from their own resources, bank loans or government grants, if available.

2 Do not have to make public their business dealings.

B Setting up in business

Whether sole trader or partnership, the basics for setting up in business are:

- permission to trade in an area (a local council licence may be needed)

- registration to pay VAT (Value Added Tax) if turnover is above a certain level

- profit and loss accounts and a balance sheet so that the business can be assessed for tax and insurance contributions

- a knowledge of health and safety laws and a willingness to obey the rules.

Q List the four basics needed to set up a business?

C Advantages and disadvantages

Sole trader

✓ makes all the decisions, keeps all the profits, has total control, low start-up costs, business flexibility, job satisfaction

✗ unlimited liability (can lose personal wealth if business fails), lack of capital, pressure of responsibility

Partnership

✓ easy to set up, expertise available through partners, greater availability of finance, shared responsibilities mean less pressure

✗ liability still rests with partners, each partner is responsible for debts of others, disagreements possible

Case study

John Taylor opened a newsagency as a sole trader in 1991 with the help of his wife. He had previously worked for a big supermarket but wanted a new challenge. It cost him £5000 to set up but he was left to work long hours when his wife fell ill. He employed an assistant manager but the shop began to lose money. The shelves were half empty and customers complained about a lack of choice. John decided to go into partnership with a friend.

Remember
Learn the pros and cons of different business types.

Q List the disadvantages for a sole trader.

PRACTICE

1 Using examples from the case study, or from your own knowledge, explain the meaning of:
   a) unlimited liability   b) partnership

2 a) Describe three advantages of being a sole trader.
   b) What reasons might explain why a third of sole traders cease trading within their first year of operation?

Use examples to help your explanation.

Ltds and plcs

THE BARE BONES

➤ There are two types of company – private limited (Ltd) and public limited (plc). Both sell shares to raise finance. Limited refers to liability.

➤ Companies differ from sole traders/partnerships in how they are run and financed, and in the risks posed to the owners.

A Companies

KEY FACTS

1 Companies are usually larger than partnerships/sole traders.

- They can be **locally based** with modest turnover or **multinational giants** with millions of shareholders and worldwide activities.

2 There are two types of company – Ltds and plcs.

- **Shareholders** own the company; they have a say in the running of the company and **share in its profits by way of annual dividends.**
- The company has its **own legal identity**, separate from that of the shareholders.

3 'Limited' in both cases refers to limited liability.

Share size decides how much profit shareholders gain, and also limits their risk of losses - they can **only lose the money they invested in the business.**

Q What is limited liability?

B Private limited company (Ltd)

KEY FACT

A Ltd is usually small to medium-sized and sells shares privately to family and friends.

1 The original **owners**, as the board of directors, **keep control.** Managers are often appointed to run the day-to-day business.

2 Money raised by selling new shares helps finance business development.

Remember
A company must satisfy customers and shareholders.

C Public limited company (plc)

KEY FACT

A plc is usually large and sells shares to the public.

1 Founders may lose control over decisions: shareholders appoint directors/managers.

2 The interests of shareholders and managers can differ - the AGM and annual report help to keep everyone informed and involved.

3 Banks and financial institutions are more prepared to finance plcs.

Q Why do plcs find it easier than Ltds to raise money?

D Setting up a company

KEY FACT

It is a similar process to set up both a Ltd and a plc, but there are more rules and regulations for a plc.

1 Company information is sent to the official registrar of companies, who grants a Certificate of Incorporation (the business gets its legal identity).

2 Shares are sold and the company starts trading.

3 A plc needs at least £50 000 of finance and must produce a prospectus of financial detail for potential shareholders.

Limited liability No-one is personally liable for company debts.

← **Ltds and plcs** →

Finance From sale of shares, bank loans, government grants.

↓

Requirements AGM; annual report for shareholders; audited accounts sent to registrar of companies and open to public scrutiny.

Remember
Plcs are private companies, not state-run.

Ltds	plcs
shares sold only to founders, relatives and friends	shares listed on Stock Exchange, sold to public
at least 1 shareholder, 1 director, 1 secretary	at least 2 shareholders, 2 directors, qualified Company Secretary
takes time to sell shares; no minimum capital	shares sold easily; minimum share capital £50 000
founders of company retain control	original owners may have little influence on decisions
less status than plc; loans more difficult	large organisation, high status, good credit rating
shareholders likely to agree on objectives	may be divisions between shareholders and managers

Q Why is an AGM and an annual report important for a company?

PRACTICE

Greens Ltd sells snacks to the public and catering trade. Shares are owned by the Green family.

1 What do the letters Ltd stand for?

2 Identify two important features of a Ltd.

3 The owners of Greens have limited liability. What does this mean?

4 Why might the Green family not want to turn the company into a plc, despite needing the money that could be raised by issuing new shares?

Co-operatives and franchises

➤ Co-operative: run by people (producers, workers, consumers) with shared business interests, for the benefit of all involved.

➤ Franchise: small traders use a well-known company's trade name; the company benefits from the experience of local managers.

A Co-operatives

KEY FACT

> Co-operatives are run by people with a shared business interest, to benefit all involved. Each participant has an equal say.

1 Workers' co-operatives

• Workers buy/set up a business then share decision making and profits - this is the most common type of co-operative.

• Each worker invests an equal amount of money.

Advantages ✓	Disadvantages ✗
Close ties with local people	Expansion may be difficult – banks often reluctant to lend
Well-motivated workforce	Possible internal disputes over decisions and financial rewards
Fosters good industrial relations	Often lack business knowledge, but unwilling to buy managerial expertise

2 Producers' co-operatives

• Producers set up a marketing and retail operation, to reduce costs and prices.

• Often founded by farmers and wine producers. Expensive machinery can be bought and shared; products are sold directly to consumers.

3 Consumers' co-operatives

• Consumers set up an organisation to bulk-buy goods, then share the profits.

Case study

The best known UK co-operative is the group which includes the Co-op Retail Society and the Co-op Bank. The retail movement, set up in Rochdale, Lancashire in the 1840s, now has over 5000 shops and a turnover in excess of £8 million.

The Rochdale Co-op established principles which have guided other consumer co-ops:

• Each member has one vote.

• Anyone can buy a share.

• Goods/services are sold at a reasonable price with profits returned to members in proportion to the amount they spend.

Remember
Co-operatives offer an alternative way of running a business.

Q What is the main difference between a co-op and a plc?

B Franchises

A franchise allows a trader to use a well-known company's trade name and enables the company to benefit from the experience of local managers.

1 The **franchisee** uses a trade name, image and even products in return for regular fees.

2 The **franchiser** can operate in many places using the experience of local managers.

3 In 1994, there were over 19 000 franchises in the UK. McDonald's, The Body Shop and Holiday Inn are some well-known examples.

4 Franchises have a better chance of establishing new businesses than sole traders, but disputes over day-to-day control can arise.

Franchiser's benefits includes	Franchisee's benefits includes
Business grows without risk of debt (franchisee responsible for debts)	Less risk during start-up
Regular income	Keep most of the profits (sometimes a percentage of income is paid to franchiser)
Less organisation and staff than if a branch was opened	Selling established product and utilising successful brand image
Keep control (including choice of franchisee)	Allows for national marketing at less expense
Franchisees are usually highly-motivated with local knowledge	Assistance and training available

Case study

Mike and Alan enjoy skateboarding and are good at making boards. They decide to set up a business in a rented workshop. They pool their money and buy some materials. Unfortunately, neither relish the task of marketing and selling the boards. After six months, they have sold only a couple to friends, are still paying rent, and have no storage room left.

Q Outline the advantages to a franchisee establishing a fast-food restaurant.

1 Outline the potential advantages to Mike and Alan in buying a franchise from a national skateboarding company.

2 What extra costs would be incurred if Mike and Alan bought a franchise?

Check carefully: is this about franchiser or franchisee?

The public sector

➤ Some organisations are so important to a nation that they are owned and controlled by the government.

➤ These public sector organisations are financed by taxes as well as by selling goods and services.

A Why public sector organisations exist

Governments run public sector organisations for a variety of reasons.

1 Security - some organisations are:

- **vital to the defence** and stability of a nation (e.g. army, police force)
- **'politically sensitive'** (e.g. arms research, disposal of nuclear waste).

2 Economic - **natural monopolies** where it makes sense to have one supplier (e.g. gas).

3 Financial - high levels of investment can put off private firms (e.g. train stations).

4 Social - some organisations provide **essential services** (e.g. education, health).

5 Organisational - co-ordinating agencies are often in the public sector. They:

- **co-ordinate activities** of private businesses (e.g. Learning and Skills Councils)
- **ensure businesses follow rules** to protect consumers (e.g. Trading Standards Authority).

Q Why are motorways run by a public sector organisation?

B Is private or public best?

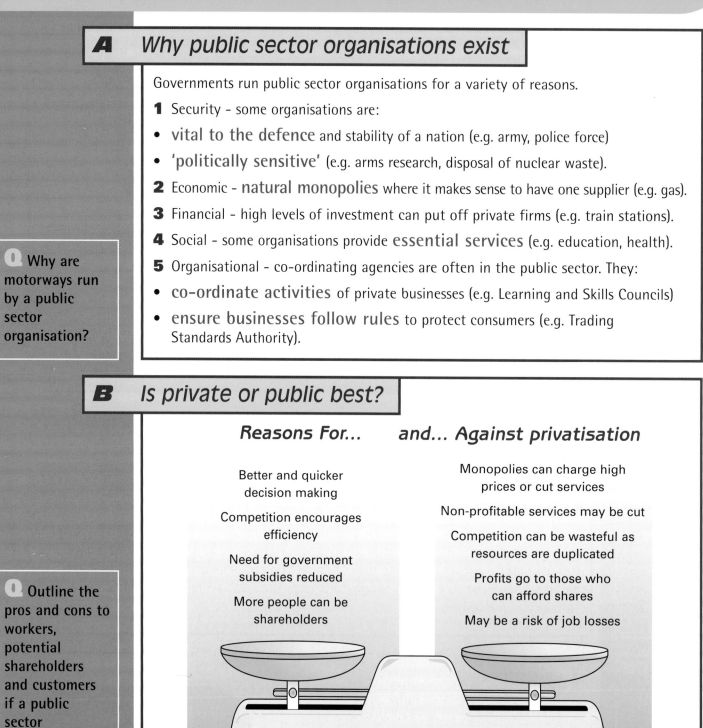

Reasons For...   **and... Against privatisation**

Better and quicker decision making

Competition encourages efficiency

Need for government subsidies reduced

More people can be shareholders

Monopolies can charge high prices or cut services

Non-profitable services may be cut

Competition can be wasteful as resources are duplicated

Profits go to those who can afford shares

May be a risk of job losses

Q Outline the pros and cons to workers, potential shareholders and customers if a public sector organisation is privatised.

C The story so far

1 In the UK, before 1979, over fifty large organisations (e.g. water, railways) were owned and run by the government. Co-ordinating one national network was thought to be more efficient than having competing businesses.

2 From 1979, successive governments have privatised many industries (e.g. BT, British Rail) - returning them to the private sector by selling shares to businesses and individuals. It was believed this increased efficiency, with government retaining some control via regulation.

3 Two more public sector organisations, the Royal Mail and London Underground, have partially privatised their activities.

D Public and private sector mixes

Most countries have public and private sector organisations. In the UK, these sectors work together in different ways.

1 Internal markets

- In the health service and local councils, departments compete against each other, and often private companies, to win contracts.

- Schools have control over their own budgets and compete for pupils in local areas.

2 Private finance

- The main services in schools, hospitals and for road maintenance are paid via taxes but if major new finance is needed, businesses can provide the money (and earn profits).

3 Quangos

- Quasi Autonomous Non-Governmental Organisations (e.g. the British Tourist Board, National Parks) are partly independent but government-funded.

Even without owning a business, governments can control business activity by making rules or supervising finances.

1 What does privatisation mean?

2 What effects can privatisation have on:
   a) the objectives of an industry?
   b) the quality of goods and services?
   c) competition and the price of products?

Business organisation

THE BARE BONES

➤ All businesses need to be organised. In simple organisations responsibilities and communication are relatively easy.

➤ Large organisations with many departments and thousands of employees will need clear communication channels and lines of responsibility.

A Organisation in small and large businesses

KEY FACT

1 In a small business communications can be direct and everyone can have a say in decisions.

- A small business (e.g. a local newsagent's) may have an owner and an assistant. Responsibility for decisions rests with the owner. The assistant may have a formal work contract, but most communications can be direct, verbal and informal.

- Communication in a small partnership can be informal, with all partners having an equal say in decisions.

KEY FACT

2 Larger businesses with more staff need a structure and more formal ways of communicating.

- Some set out to be **democratic** and **share responsibility** for decisions across the business. There may be internal **structures based on groups** with common interests, or on friendship groups.

- Most have a **hierarchical culture**, with decisions **handed down to the many, from the few at the top.**

KEY FACT

3 Hierarchical organisations have a clear chain of command from the most senior to junior staff.

```
          owners
         directors
         managers
        supervisors
        operatives
```

- At each level, people take orders and instructions from above and give them to those below. Requests and complaints are sent upwards.

- Communications reflect the formal business culture, with many written notices and memos, formal reports, and meetings with written agendas and minutes.

Q How does a manager of a large company find out about problems on the factory floor?

- It is thorough and detailed but may be expensive and time-consuming. Electronic communications have helped speed up and save money on formal communications.

B Organisation charts

1 Large businesses organise themselves in different ways.

The most common forms of organisation are:

- by **function** (based on people's roles, e.g. marketing, finance)
- by **product** (separate departments for each product, e.g. Ford vans, cars)
- by **geographical area** (local branches or national divisions, e.g. Ford UK, Ford Spain).

A typical organisation chart, showing a business divided up by function:

Q Produce an organisation chart for your school/college. Explain differences in the span of control for the Heads of English and Year 9.

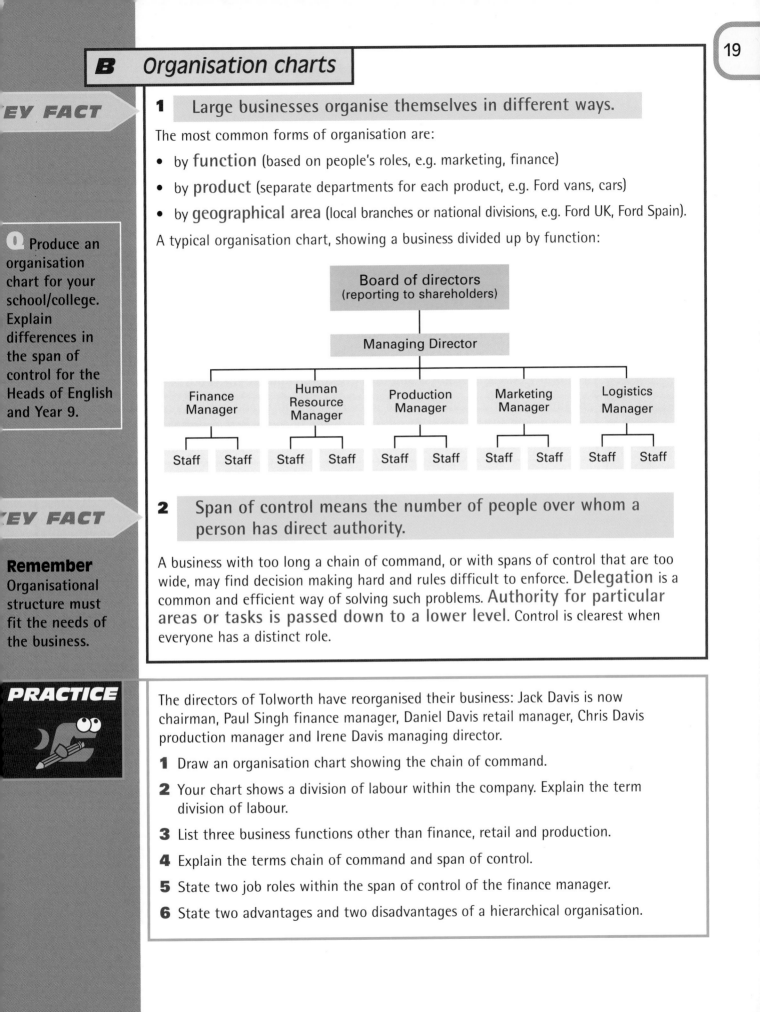

```
                    Board of directors
                  (reporting to shareholders)
                           |
                    Managing Director
                           |
  ┌──────────┬──────────┬──────────┬──────────┬──────────┐
Finance    Human      Production  Marketing   Logistics
Manager    Resource   Manager     Manager     Manager
           Manager
  |          |           |           |           |
Staff Staff Staff Staff Staff Staff Staff Staff Staff Staff
```

2 Span of control means the number of people over whom a person has direct authority.

A business with too long a chain of command, or with spans of control that are too wide, may find decision making hard and rules difficult to enforce. **Delegation** is a common and efficient way of solving such problems. **Authority for particular areas or tasks is passed down to a lower level.** Control is clearest when everyone has a distinct role.

Remember
Organisational structure must fit the needs of the business.

PRACTICE

The directors of Tolworth have reorganised their business: Jack Davis is now chairman, Paul Singh finance manager, Daniel Davis retail manager, Chris Davis production manager and Irene Davis managing director.

1 Draw an organisation chart showing the chain of command.

2 Your chart shows a division of labour within the company. Explain the term division of labour.

3 List three business functions other than finance, retail and production.

4 Explain the terms chain of command and span of control.

5 State two job roles within the span of control of the finance manager.

6 State two advantages and two disadvantages of a hierarchical organisation.

Business objectives

THE BARE BONES

➤ Business objectives show what a business aims to achieve.
➤ A business's success can be measured in terms of meeting these targets.
➤ Different stakeholders may have different objectives for a business.

A Types of business objectives

KEY FACT

Businesses can pursue three broad objectives (or aims).

1 **To make a profit** - the key concern for most private businesses.

2 **To provide a service** - the objective for most public sector businesses (e.g. schools, hospitals). They usually aim to break even.

3 **To be charitable** - some businesses solely aim to help others. They operate as any efficient business and often have to compete for funds.

Business objectives can be found in company reports and publicity materials. These provide a statement of purpose for the business and are often referred to as a **mission statement**.

Q What is a mission statement?

B More detailed objectives and targets

Within these general headings, businesses set themselves more detailed objectives. Examples of these, and ways they might be achieved, are shown below:

1 to **maximise profits**, by charging the highest possible prices (a chocolate firm charges a high price for luxury chocolates)

2 to win a **larger share of the market**, by taking over a rival business (a French car company takes over a British firm to increase sales in the UK)

3 to ensure **long term survival**, by borrowing money to invest in developing new products (an international airline borrows money to buy jets for long-haul flights)

4 to ensure **services reach those in most need**, by restricting them to a named group at a time (a hospital targets emergency treatment for elderly heart patients).

Once established, these objectives are documented in fine detail, and targets are set (e.g. a certain increase in profit by a set date).
To be of use in measuring success, these targets must be SMART.

S pecific
M easurable
A ttainable
R ealistic
T imed

Q Name five objectives that a major retailer might set itself for the year ahead.

C   Striking a balance

Businesses need to strike a balance between their objectives.

Different businesses give their objectives different levels of importance.

1 The most important objective for many private businesses is profit, but not at any price. Some businesses are keen to maintain customer satisfaction and a reputation for quality.

2 Businesses may accept a drop in profits or sales to keep their independence.

3 Some objectives are measurable and short term, like profit; others are more general and long term, such as independence.

4 Public sector businesses aim to provide a good service, with high levels of customer satisfaction and efficient use of resources. However, they must also meet tight financial targets.

Q Compare similarities and differences in objectives of a charity shop and an independent grocer.

D   Stakeholders' objectives

Stakeholders are groups that have an interest in the success of a business.

Their objectives often vary:

Remember
Stakeholders' objectives can overlap but may sometimes be conflicting.

Local community: Local jobs, clean environment.

Suppliers: Repeat orders, reliable payment of bills.

Customers: Value for money, choice.

Business

Managers: Best salary, status for department.

Employees: Job satisfaction, good pay.

Owners: Survival in business, best return on investment.

Q List four stakeholders of a company.

PRACTICE

Ragbags Ltd makes and sells children's clothes in the north of England. The managers want to increase sales in the south, by opening several new stores. But some shareholders are worried that the new investment will affect profitability.

1 Why might the managers want to increase sales?

2 Why might some shareholders be more interested in keeping profits high?

3 How might expansion affect customers?

4 How could the managers persuade shareholders to support the proposed expansion?

Beware the difference between shareholder and stakeholder.

Business production

THE BARE BONES
➤ Business production covers the whole process from research to sales.
➤ Businesses may produce one product or sell a wide product mix.
➤ Large scale production may cut costs for some businesses.

A Business production

KEY FACT **1** Business production describes the whole process.

- The process begins with an idea for a new product. Research may suggest the best way of making or supplying the item. Investors provide capital for equipment, materials etc. Finally, the finished product is marketed, distributed and sold to customers.

KEY FACT **2** Business production involves the use of different resources.

- Materials: use of land, extraction of **raw materials**, materials from other businesses.
- Workers: a **labour** force is needed, in the UK or abroad.
- **Capital**: investment in machinery, buildings, vehicles.
- **Enterprise**: the owner(s) take the risk that the business will be a success.

KEY FACT **3** Business production can be product-led or customer-led.

- In the past, businesses often made **products first**, then tried to sell them.
- Now, most businesses are **customer-led** (or market-led, see page 60). Customer **preferences** are **researched** and products identified that will satisfy them. A business then tries to **make the products**, keeping **costs below the price** customers would be willing to pay. This may mean finding new production methods and using large-scale processes.

Q How do product-led and customer-led firms differ?

B Product choice

KEY FACT Businesses may sell one product or have a wide product mix.

1 Sole product businesses (e.g. a beef farmer):
  ✓ Good if the product is a quality one and hard to obtain.
  ✗ Can be risky if demand for the product suddenly falls.
2 Businesses with a wide product range (e.g. a motor company):
  ✓ Customers have greater choice; the business spreads its risks.
  ✗ Can be difficult to manage on a large scale while keeping down costs.
3 Businesses with a wide product mix (e.g. Unilever):
  ✓ Risks are spread across many products in different markets.
  ✗ Can be difficult to manage products outside the business's core activity.

B

Businesses need to assess their products' performance.

The Boston Matrix provides a framework to assess sales growth and market share.

	High	Market share	Low
Fast	⭐⭐⭐ **'Stars'**		**? 'Question Marks'**
Market growth	Likely to give good cash returns; need a lot of advertising		Difficult to be sure of their future; need lots of investment
Slow	🐄 **'Cash Cows'**		🐕 **'Dogs'**
	Steady market; well-set products which can be 'milked' for profits		Poor market share; need to be killed off

Q Why might a car company want a range of models in its product mix?

C   Scale of production

1   Small firms can have <u>higher costs</u> but better service.

- Producing goods on a small scale, fixed costs per product unit are high.
- Can offer **personal and local service** and **specialist products**.
- Can offer **flexibility** in meeting different demands.

2   Larger firms can take advantage of <u>economies of scale</u>.

Economies of scale (reductions in unit costs when producing larger quantities) may be:

- **Technical** - large firms can use machinery more effectively.
- **Trading** - large firms can buy in bulk at favourable prices.
- **Financial** - large firms can usually borrow more at lower interest rates.
- **Managerial** - large firms can hire specialist highly-skilled management.

3   Firms may become <u>too large to manage efficiently</u>.

- For example, a firm with many factories nationwide may develop **communications problems**, leading to **inefficiency** and **increased costs**.

Q Why can a small specialist bakers survive alongside a larger supermarket in the same shopping centre?

PRACTICE

1 In what ways are supermarkets customer-led?

2 Explain how supermarkets benefit from economies of scale.

Several ideas with examples are better than one long point.

THE BARE BONES
➤ Businesses may choose a mix of job, batch and flow production methods.

➤ Just-in-time production can be efficient if carefully managed.

A Choosing a production method

KEY FACT

> Most businesses use a mix of production methods.

1 Job production: making a unique item from start to finish, e.g. house extension, ship.

- Often a response to an individual order.

2 Batch production: larger-scale production of 'batches' of similar items, e.g. bread, clothing.

- An entire batch of products is processed through a production stage before moving to the next stage.

- Machinery is reset and a new batch of different items is then processed.

- Production is aimed at the market rather than the individual customer.

3 Flow (or mass) production: Continuous production of identical items, e.g. newspapers, cars.

- The items flow through a set of specialised operations on an assembly line.

- Division of labour is essential, with workers trained to do specialist tasks.

- Production is aimed at the largest markets of all.

Remember
Businesses often combine different production methods when making a range of products.

	Advantages	Disadvantages
Job production	High quality product made by skilled workers Job satisfaction high Easy to isolate problem areas	Expensive materials Expensive labour Slow process, machinery often idle Repeat orders unlikely
Batch production	Lower unit costs (increased scale of production) Flexibility possible in batch quantity, according to demand More specialised machinery with less idle time	Costly storage needed Some repetition in jobs Batches need to be moved Machinery needs resetting
Flow production	Large output, low unit cost Good use of production time Low-skilled, easily-trained labour Products of standard quality	Large investment in machinery Inflexible assembly line Repetitive work, poor motivation Products all the same Breakdowns cause big problems

Q What production method might be used to make a range of cakes for a supermarket?

B Just-in-time (JIT) production

EY FACT

Just-in-time production is an efficient method if carefully managed.

✓

- JIT production is a relatively new development.
- Raw materials, parts and components are made available in just the right quantity.
- Each load arrives at the assembly line, fully quality-checked, just in time to be used.
- Computer-controlled information links are a vital part of the process.
- Can save time and money usually spent on storage/internal stock movement.

✗

- JIT needs very careful management and close ties with suppliers.
- Breakdowns in the system can cause costly delays.

Remember
JIT methods won't suit every business.

Q What might be the pros and cons of using JIT for a large furniture maker?

C Teamwork

EY FACT

In most production processes, teamwork is essential.

1 In batch or flow production, teams typically take charge of sections of the process.

2 The team controls the speed and quality of production.

3 The team can help to spot and sort out problems.

4 Greater job satisfaction can be gained if proper training is received.

5 Some computer-controlled processes have led to less teamwork, more part-time work, less job security and less satisfaction.

Q Give three benefits of using teamwork in production.

PRACTICE

Crown Fashions Ltd makes clothes for major high street stores. The stores require a range of sizes, colours and designs for each garment. To meet these requirements, Crown uses batch production methods.

1 What is batch production?

2 Why are batch production methods well suited to the manufacture of clothing?

Remember to match each advantage you mention with an example from clothing manufacture.

Efficiency and new technology

THE BARE BONES

➤ A business must be efficient to compete successfully.

➤ Efficiency can be increased by innovation and the use of new technology in the production process.

A — Business efficiency

KEY FACT ▶

1 In a competitive world, a business must produce maximum output at minimum cost. This is known as efficient production.

- Efficiency is a measure of how well the production process is running.
- With some products, it is easy to measure the number produced by a worker or machine in a certain time.
- It is more difficult to measure efficiency when a business produces a service. Quality may be more important than quantity.
- Improvements in efficiency of production can come from automation (greater use of machinery), changing work practices and productivity deals with workers.
- A firm may need to invest in management training or reorganisation to become more efficient.

KEY FACT ▶

2 Different measures of efficiency are used by businesses.

1 **Productivity** e.g. output per team, per person, per man-hour, per machine.

2 **Unit costs** Total costs divided by quantity produced.
- Falling unit costs: good sign of improving efficiency.
- Rising unit costs: production costs up or fewer products made.

3 **Idle resources** e.g. machines and workers standing idle.
  Can be improved:
- by changing work practices
- by mechanisation
- by use of part-time workers.

4 **Stock levels**
- Too few stocks can lead to stoppages in production.
- Too many stocks can lead to surplus goods that no one wants.

5 **Product quality** as measured by complaints or number of products returned to a business.

6 **Poor management** e.g. evidence of inefficiencies right across the factory.

Remember
The comment 'this business is inefficient' needs careful explanation.

Q How could you measure a school's efficiency?

B Computer technology in business production

1 Computer controlled technology has made big improvements in some industries.

There are several different uses of computers in business production.

1 CAM (computer-aided manufacturing):

- In processes such as engineering, computers program machines.
- They complete work more accurately and for longer than humans.
- Robots are ideal for dangerous, dirty or heavy jobs.

2 CAD (computer-aided design):

- Products can now be designed on screen using complex 3-D models.
- Production processes can be planned in advance.
- Saves expensive research time; avoids costly mistakes.

3 CIM (computer-integrated manufacturing):

- CIM factories combine all the latest technological developments.
- Everything is controlled by computers.
- The computer programming team replaces the old factory managers.
- Products can be made on a large scale but 'custom made' in assembly to meet individual customer needs.

Remember
New technology can lead to job losses, but can mean lower prices, more demand and new jobs.

Q What is the main difference between CAM and CIM?

2 Computer technology has costs and benefits.

- High investment costs can be covered by cutting labour costs.
- Benefits depend on selling large quantities of the product and on how long the technology stays up to date.

PRACTICE

Beau Nurseries employs four production staff, three sales staff and ten part-timers, some on a seasonal basis. The company plans to expand and introduce automation, CAM and computer control systems into the hothouses in order to become more capital-intensive.

1 State the meaning of:
a) automation   b) CAM   c) computer control systems

2 How could these new technologies be used in the hothouses?

3 Explain the meaning of the term 'capital-intensive'.

4 How might the new technology affect the work of Beau employees?

In questions such as no. 4, remember to include any disadvantages as well as advantages.

Quality management

THE BARE BONES

➤ Product quality is determined by businesses, their customers and the law.

➤ There are traditional and modern ways of managing quality production.

A Deciding on the quality of a product

KEY FACT

1 The quality of a product depends on its purpose.

All goods have to meet a purpose. Some, e.g. parachutes, need to be totally reliable. For others, e.g. clothes, appearance may be more important than quality.

KEY FACT

2 Product quality is determined by businesses, customers and the law.

1 Businesses have different approaches to quality. They may try to make the best possible product or may want to compete on price.

2 Customers may expect a product to: last a long time; be fashionable in design; offer good back-up services from the producer; offer reasonable value for money.

3 The quality of a product can be set by law. Some products, e.g. car safety belts, must pass research checks before they can be sold. National standards are checked and enforced by government. All products must be fit for purpose as advertised at the point of sale.

Q What might happen if a designer sweatshirt failed to meet your expectations?

B Traditional quality control

KEY FACT

1 Traditional quality control methods rely on sample checks by a specialist department.

Traditionally, the quality control department has been seen as responsible for improving and maintaining product quality. This includes monitoring machine performance, checking the quality of bought-in supplies and analysing the use of manpower.

2 Research and Development departments (R & D) help develop new, high quality products.

R & D involves scientific research for new ideas/products. Many projects never reach a development stage. It takes time and money but may save costs in the long term. Usually only large, specialised companies can afford their own R & D departments.

Q How would the quality of sweatshirts be checked in a traditional factory using mass production?

C *Modern quality control*

> Businesses are increasingly using a system of total quality management (TQM) which makes all employees responsible for quality.

- New quality systems involve all staff in an overall 'quality policy'.
- The policy aims at 'zero defects' and tries to meet customers' needs.
- A modern quality management process cannot just be 'stuck on' to an old system.
- Good teamwork is required: a business with an open decision-making process finds the move to TQM much easier than those without.
- A top quality process should: lead to good quality products; allow workers to operate safely; protect the environment; cut down waste.

Remember
Quality management needs planning, training and, often, a change in production methods.

Q What does Kaizen mean?

Traditional methods	Modern methods
Post-production quality control: controller randomly checks finished goods. Wasteful, as faults are only found at the end.	TQM: everyone involved in the process. Improves staff motivation. Faults spotted/sorted out quickly. Costs are involved, though, as workers must be educated/trained to measure and monitor quality and seek improvement.
Process control: controller samples products throughout the production process. Slight improvement.	Kaizen: a Japanese idea of continual improvement. Workers suggest improvements as often as possible so potential concerns are dealt with before they become problems. Voluntary groups ('quality circles') meet often to discuss ways of improving work and production.

PRACTICE

GRC employs seventy workers at its main factory making plastic moulded products for kitchens. All their products are made from plastic granules, which are melted and put into moulds. This process is computer controlled. On the other side of town, GRC has a smaller factory with a supervisor and six people employed in assembly and packaging.

1 GRC is considering moving assembly and packaging on to the main site. Do you think this is a good idea? Give reasons.

2 The production manager believes everyone should be involved in quality control.
   a) What is meant by quality control?
   b) Describe ways in which GRC might try to obtain a high standard of quality control.

Business location

THE BARE BONES

➤ A business chooses its location for many reasons, including economic and legal ones.

➤ The best location is often the result of a trade-off between different factors.

A Factors affecting business location

1 Labour

A business requiring a highly skilled workforce needs to be in an area linked to the industry or one with local training facilities.

A business looking for mainly unskilled, cheap labour looks for an area with a plentiful supply; low costs of transporting staff; and where staff can be persuaded to relocate.

2 Raw materials and the market

Firms dealing with perishable goods (e.g. canning and freezing firms) need to locate near to where the goods are produced.

Businesses whose process is bulk-reducing (e.g. brickmakers, a sawmill) locate near to the source of materials, to reduce transport costs.

Bulk-increasing businesses (e.g. car manufacturers) locate close to the market.

3 Land

The amount and cost of land will affect choice.

The nature of the land may be important (e.g. chemical plants need large, flat sites, which can bear heavy loads). A site in bad condition needs more investment.

Local planning restrictions must be considered.

4 Infrastructure and services

All businesses need: good sources of energy and water; efficient drainage and waste disposal; good communications; fast, efficient transport links.

Locating to a remote, undeveloped site means paying to link up to such systems.

5 Other influences

Climate.

Competition and/or co-operation with other businesses.

Government/pressure group influence.

Remember
The reasons for location may be unique to a business or to its owner.

Q What factors would influence the location of a factory making fish fingers and other frozen foods?

B Government and pressure groups

Government and private pressure groups can influence where a business locates.

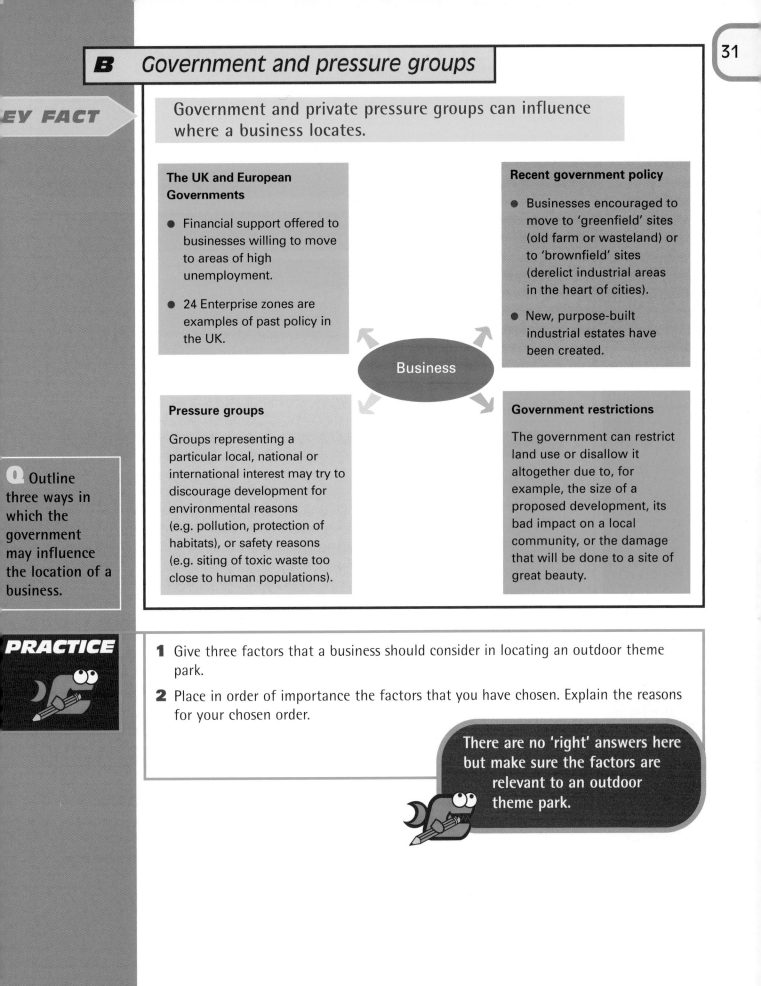

The UK and European Governments

- Financial support offered to businesses willing to move to areas of high unemployment.

- 24 Enterprise zones are examples of past policy in the UK.

Recent government policy

- Businesses encouraged to move to 'greenfield' sites (old farm or wasteland) or to 'brownfield' sites (derelict industrial areas in the heart of cities).

- New, purpose-built industrial estates have been created.

Business

Pressure groups

Groups representing a particular local, national or international interest may try to discourage development for environmental reasons (e.g. pollution, protection of habitats), or safety reasons (e.g. siting of toxic waste too close to human populations).

Government restrictions

The government can restrict land use or disallow it altogether due to, for example, the size of a proposed development, its bad impact on a local community, or the damage that will be done to a site of great beauty.

Q Outline three ways in which the government may influence the location of a business.

PRACTICE

1 Give three factors that a business should consider in locating an outdoor theme park.

2 Place in order of importance the factors that you have chosen. Explain the reasons for your chosen order.

There are no 'right' answers here but make sure the factors are relevant to an outdoor theme park.

Business finance

THE BARE BONES

➤ Financial planning, costings, forecasts and accounts are essential to manage and judge the success of a business.

➤ Sources of finance can come from inside the business (internal) or outside (external).

A Importance of finance and financial management

KEY FACT

1 Finance is essential to any business.

Business owners need money to pay for:

- the **start-up costs** of buildings, equipment and materials
- the regular **running costs** such as electricity bills, employees' wages and taxes
- **unexpected events** such as breakdowns in equipment or accidents
- **investment** in new equipment or building expansion.

KEY FACT

2 Good financial management is essential to a business's survival.

- A good **business plan** must be written to back up a request for a loan.
- Estimates need to be made of the point at which a business will **break even** and what will be a **reasonable price** to charge for a product.
- Regular **cash flow forecasts and budgets** help to keep the business afloat on a month-by-month and year-by-year basis.
- **Detailed accounts** help managers to judge the success of the business activities.

Remember
Business finance involves the interpretation of figures.

Case study

Mark and Megan have a sandwich business called Double M's. They rent a unit on a business park and sell directly to shops and local firms, offering working lunches.

When they first formed the business, they thought about all their start-up costs and their ongoing running costs. They decided how much money they needed to set up, and took a plan to the bank in case they needed a loan.

Mark and Megan make regular detailed costings, working out their costs and measuring them against revenue. These calculations show their break-even point and help them to set a price for their products, to give them a reasonable profit. They produce monthly cash flow forecasts which show them if they have the cash to pay monthly bills. They draw up business accounts to show how the figures work.

With all the details in front of them, Mark and Megan can measure the performance of their business and determine whether it is making a reasonable profit, or whether adjustments need to be made.

Q How do business and personal finances differ?

B   Sources of finance

Finance for a business can come from a variety of sources.

Some sources of finance are better for start-up costs; some are better for other costs, such as running costs. Financial sources can be grouped in different ways:

- by time period (short term or long term)
- whether the finance comes from inside the business (internal) or outside (external).

The table below compares internal and external sources of finance and their main use.

Source	Features	Used for
Internal		
Retained profit	Money saved out of net profit. No interest to pay; easily available. Most common source of finance.	Running costs. Also, potentially, renewal, expansion.
Investment	Money put in by owners or, if a limited company, obtained by selling shares. Usually long-term commitment.	Start-up costs, buying equipment, renewal, expansion.
Selling / leasing assets	A one-off for raising money, generally when a business is struggling.	Buying equipment, emergency running costs.
External		
Bank overdrafts	Money allowed to be withdrawn, despite account having negative balance. Short-term agreements, high interest charged.	Covering gaps in cash flow.
Loans	Money from banks etc. Arranged over different time periods; interest charged. Often need guarantees to ensure pay-back.	Start-up costs, buying equipment.
Grants	Money from government, generally tied in to fixed commitments such as improving a region's unemployment or environment.	Start-up costs, buying equipment, expansion.
Trade credit	Buying goods, but not paying for them until an agreed later date.	Buying stock.
Hire purchase (HP)	HP or leasing payments spread over time, so less money committed in the short term. With HP, interest charged, but item eventually owned outright. With leasing, item never owned but can be updated/ repaired easily.	Buying equipment, renewal.

Q What might be the best methods of finance for starting a business?

PRACTICE

1 Give three examples of internal and three of external sources of finance.

2 Why might restaurant owners seek a bank loan to pay for a second restaurant?

Financial planning

THE BARE BONES

➤ Different kinds of business costs can be financed in different ways.
➤ A business plan is central to good financial planning. It shows information and figures which predict the future performance of the business.

A Different kinds of business costs

KEY FACT

Different kinds of finance are used to cover different business costs.

1 Start-up costs are financed by start-up capital.

2 Running and renewal costs are financed by working capital.

3 Expansion costs are financed by investment.

1 Start-up costs: costs of buying a first stock of materials, equipment, e.g. cars, computers, specialist machines and maybe purchase of premises.

Start-up capital

Working capital

2 Running costs: regular costs of producing goods or services, e.g. wages, insurance, electricity, raw materials, rent of premises and, possibly, machinery and petrol for vehicles.

3 Renewal costs: costs of repairing and replacing equipment and premises.

4 Expansion costs: costs of installing more production lines, employing new staff, opening new premises, developing a new product etc.

Investment

Q List the costs for Mark and Megan's sandwich business and sort into three groups: start-up; running; renewal.

B Business plans

1 A business plan is central to good financial planning. It shows the information and figures which predict future performance of the business.

- A business plan plays a vital role in financial planning, especially if other organisations, such as banks, are to be asked for loans.
- It is a formal, detailed document, which explains how the finance for a business is going to be raised.
- It contains a cash flow and other financial forecasts.
- It shows how soon the business is likely to break even.
- It includes background information (e.g. product/service offered, number of staff, target market).
- It shows the targets being set (the business objectives).

Remember
Finance involves risks for business owners and for lenders. Will the possible profit outweigh the risk?

2 A business plan provides different kinds of information for different stakeholders.

It helps managers:
- to avoid costly mistakes
- to set targets for review
- by providing financial guidelines.

It provides vital information for lenders:
- The clarity of the managers' planning.
- The length of time it will probably take to repay the loan.
- The risks of the business venture.

Q Why are good business plans important?

PRACTICE

1 A group of 18-year-olds ask you, a bank manager, for a £5000 loan to help start a mobile disco business. They hope to be in profit after a year. What information would you expect to see in their business plan? If you loaned the money, what rules would you make for repayment?

2 For each of the following situations, explain which source of finance would be most useful:
a) A business that wishes to finance a major land purchase for a new factory.
b) A small taxi firm that needs to buy a new vehicle.
c) A business that wants to take over a neighbouring building to add to its rented area, and use it to store more stock.

Break even

THE BARE BONES
- ➤ General running costs can be divided into fixed and variable costs.
- ➤ A break-even point can be found where revenue just covers costs.
- ➤ Break-even analysis helps a business to make decisions about prices, costs and the level of sales.

A Fixed and variable costs

KEY FACT

1 Businesses can divide general running costs into fixed and variable costs.

- Fixed costs (overheads) do not, in the short term, change with the number of goods or services produced, e.g. rent on buildings, rates to local councils, interest on loans.
  (NB if the business shrinks or expands drastically, then fixed costs will change.)

- Variable costs change with the amount of goods or services produced, e.g. cost of raw materials, parts, packaging.

KEY FACT

2 Some costs may be classified differently by different businesses.

Some costs (e.g. electricity, transport, wages) may be fixed costs for one business but variable costs for another. For example, power for a high street bank is a fixed cost, but for a launderette is a variable cost dependent on use of the washing machines. Over a longer period all costs could vary.

Q Give examples of fixed and variable costs for a bus firm.

B Calculating the break-even point

KEY FACT

1 Fixed and variable costs are measured against sales revenue to calculate whether a business will make a loss, profit, or break even at different levels of sales.

KEY FACT

2 There are two commonly used ways to work out the break-even point.

1 The contribution method involves a two-part calculation:
  a) price per unit - variable cost per unit (variable cost) = contribution (to cover fixed costs)
  b) Break-even point (level of sales) = fixed costs divided by contribution

2 The graph method involves drawing lines to show costs at different outputs and expected revenue from different levels of sales. Break even is at the point where the lines cross.

Q If fixed costs = £2000, variable costs = £8 per unit, price = £10 a unit, what level of sales is needed to break even?

B

a) Plot fixed costs (horizontal line at level of fixed costs). Then plot variable costs (diagonal line showing costs at different outputs)

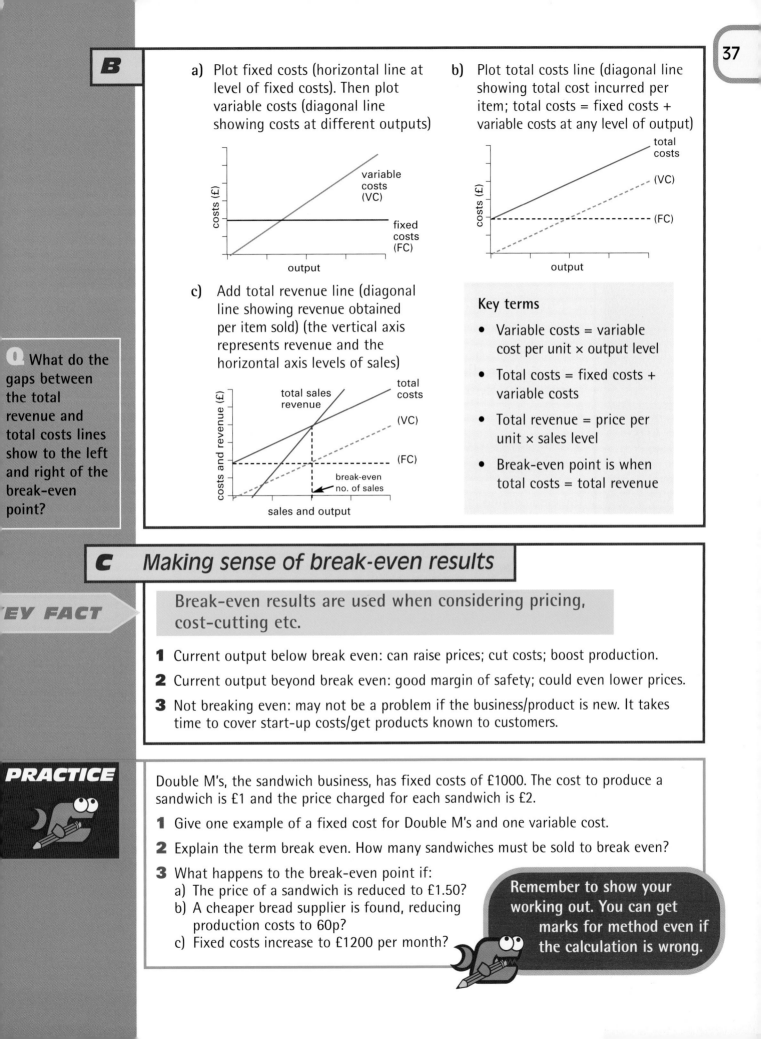

b) Plot total costs line (diagonal line showing total cost incurred per item; total costs = fixed costs + variable costs at any level of output)

c) Add total revenue line (diagonal line showing revenue obtained per item sold) (the vertical axis represents revenue and the horizontal axis levels of sales)

Q What do the gaps between the total revenue and total costs lines show to the left and right of the break-even point?

Key terms

- Variable costs = variable cost per unit × output level
- Total costs = fixed costs + variable costs
- Total revenue = price per unit × sales level
- Break-even point is when total costs = total revenue

C Making sense of break-even results

EY FACT

Break-even results are used when considering pricing, cost-cutting etc.

1 Current output below break even: can raise prices; cut costs; boost production.

2 Current output beyond break even: good margin of safety; could even lower prices.

3 Not breaking even: may not be a problem if the business/product is new. It takes time to cover start-up costs/get products known to customers.

PRACTICE

Double M's, the sandwich business, has fixed costs of £1000. The cost to produce a sandwich is £1 and the price charged for each sandwich is £2.

1 Give one example of a fixed cost for Double M's and one variable cost.

2 Explain the term break even. How many sandwiches must be sold to break even?

3 What happens to the break-even point if:
  a) The price of a sandwich is reduced to £1.50?
  b) A cheaper bread supplier is found, reducing production costs to 60p?
  c) Fixed costs increase to £1200 per month?

Remember to show your working out. You can get marks for method even if the calculation is wrong.

Cash flow

THE BARE BONES
➤ A business needs enough cash to cover its immediate needs.
➤ A cash flow forecast predicts money coming in and going out over a fixed period.

A Why cash is important

KEY FACT

1 A business needs enough money to cover its immediate needs.

- **Cash** in the bank is **a liquid asset** that allows a firm to buy the goods and services it needs, add value to them, trade and make profits.

- A firm might be making profits, but if it does not have enough cash to pay its **creditors (people it owes)**, it can be declared **insolvent** by the courts and may have to cease trading.

- Every year thousands of businesses fail as a result of cash flow problems.

KEY FACT

2 Cash flows can be compared to water flowing into and out of a bath.

The cash coming in is like water from a tap. Cash going out is like water out of the plughole. The task is to keep a reasonable level of water in the bath.

Cash in
Start-up capital; cash from sales of goods/services; bank loans; grants etc.

Cash out
Raw materials or stock; fixed costs; tax payments; equipment; wages/salaries etc.

Q Why might a Christmas decorations manufacturer have a cash shortage in the summer?

B Cash flow forecasts

1 A cash flow forecast is a way of predicting cash in and cash out over a fixed period.

Generally a chart or graph, a cash flow enables established businesses to check whether or not a cash crisis is looming. It is also vital to the business plan presented by a new company to a potential lender. On a chart, cash inflows (receipts) are listed first, followed by cash outflows (payments).

Remember
Profit is a surplus from trading activities. Cash is an asset that can be used to pay debts.

B

2 Interpretation of a cash flow chart is important for a business.

- Negative closing balance (a deficit): indicates not enough cash to pay the bills.
- Regular large surplus: suggests the business could repay some debts or buy new stocks or equipment.
- Credit sales: payment for goods/services is not received until some time after the sale.
- Buying goods on credit: goods arrive before payment is due.

Here is a cash flow forecast chart of a company with an opening January balance of £0:

	January	February	March	April
Cash in	9500	7000	4000	4000
minus **Cash out**	7400	6500	6600	5500
equals **Net cash flow**	2100	500	-2600	-1500
plus **Opening balance**	0	2100	2600	0
equals **Closing balance**	2100	2600	0	-1500

Q What does this chart tell you about the cash flow for January to April? If this business is to be successful in the months ahead, what must happen to the net cash flow during May to December?

PRACTICE

A soft toy company, Fuzz, has drawn up an actual cash flow graph for the last six months' trading, to compare with its forecast for the same period.

1 What does the cash flow forecast graph show?

2 How did the actual cash flow differ from the forecast?

3 What problems might these differences cause for Fuzz?

4 How might Fuzz improve its cash flow?

Financial statements

➤ A business's financial accounts are records of all its financial transactions.

➤ The profit and loss account and balance sheet are the two main financial statements.

A   The importance of financial accounts

KEY FACT

All businesses need an efficient system for keeping track of their money.

The profit and loss account and the balance sheet are the two main financial statements.

• Both provide information on recent business activity.

• Both show how these activities have been paid for.

• This information can be compared with figures from previous years to assist decision making about the future.

• Small firms draw up their own financial statements or pay an accountant to do it.

• Larger companies have their own finance department.

• By law, all companies must provide shareholders with accounting information.

• Public limited companies do this through the annual report and accounts.

Q How does a large business keep track of its money?

B   Profit and loss account

Q Which stakeholders would be interested in the profit and loss account and why?

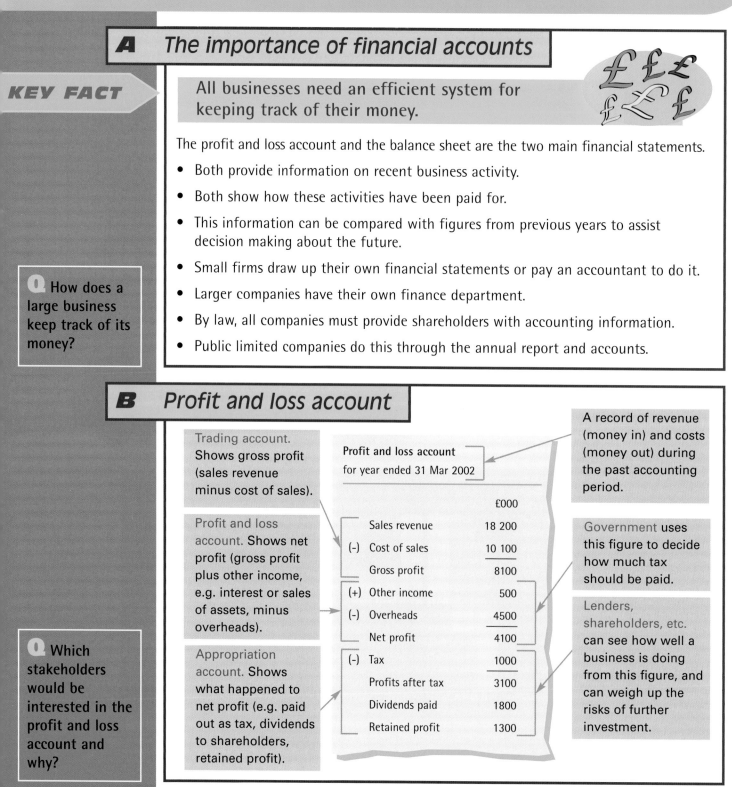

Trading account. Shows gross profit (sales revenue minus cost of sales).

Profit and loss account. Shows net profit (gross profit plus other income, e.g. interest or sales of assets, minus overheads).

Appropriation account. Shows what happened to net profit (e.g. paid out as tax, dividends to shareholders, retained profit).

A record of revenue (money in) and costs (money out) during the past accounting period.

Government uses this figure to decide how much tax should be paid.

Lenders, shareholders, etc. can see how well a business is doing from this figure, and can weigh up the risks of further investment.

Profit and loss account for year ended 31 Mar 2002

		£000
	Sales revenue	18 200
(-)	Cost of sales	10 100
	Gross profit	8100
(+)	Other income	500
(-)	Overheads	4500
	Net profit	4100
(-)	Tax	1000
	Profits after tax	3100
	Dividends paid	1800
	Retained profit	1300

C Balance sheet

A record of the value of what a firm owns (its assets), what it owes (its liabilities) and the value of the capital invested in the firm. It is a 'snapshot' taken at a particular point in time (usually the last day of the accounting period).

Assets (e.g. buildings and equipment). May be different views of how much such things are worth.

Assets which are easily turned into cash.

Debts to be repaid within one year (e.g. short-term loans).

Current assets minus current liabilities.

Total assets minus current liabilities.

Remember
Assets are all the things a business owns; liabilities are what it 'owes'.

Long-term loans, etc. Balance sheet layout varies between firms - these liabilities, instead of being subtracted here, are often added to the capital and reserves section below.

Q What figure tells you about a business's ability to pay its debts in the short term?

Owners' or share capital, retained profit, loans, grants etc.

Balance sheet
as at 31 Mar 2002

	£000	£000
Assets		
Fixed assets		3400
Current assets		
Stock	800	
Debtors	2100	
Cash	2300	
	5200	
Liabilities		
Current liabilities	3800	
Net current assets (working capital)		1400
Net assets employed		4800
Long-term liabilities	1800	
		3000
Capital & reserves		
Share capital		1700
Retained profit		1300
Capital employed		3000

These figures must balance: the 'where is the money now' and 'where did the money come from' boxes must tally.

PRACTICE

You are an accountant. A friend asks you about financial statements. Can you answer their questions (below)?

1 What will tell us whether or not we can pay off our debts?

2 What will tell us whether or not we can expand?

Think which figures inform you about the short-term position and which tell you about the longer term.

Financial performance

THE BARE BONES

➤ Managers can check on financial performance by taking the accounts information for the past year and doing some comparisons and investigations with the figures.

➤ Detailed information on financial performance is provided by performance ratios.

A   The importance of performance ratios

KEY FACT

Businesses should always be aware of the condition of their finances, so they can make any necessary adjustments to keep afloat.

- Managers need to have more precise knowledge about a company's profitability and liquidity than just whether it is making money and whether it has enough cash to pay off its debts.

- Managers might need to know if it is making enough money given the level of sales or money invested.

- They might need to know what percentage of available cash would be needed to pay off its debts.

- This detailed information is provided by performance ratios.

- Ratios are worked out by comparing different pairs of figures in the accounts that are related in some way.

- Each ratio gives slightly different information about the profitability or liquidity of a business.

Remember
Ratios are based on past figures. They can help with forecasts but will not guarantee results.

Which of these two companies has the better performance?

	Sales	Profits
Company A	£10 million	£1 million
Company B	£200 million	£8 million

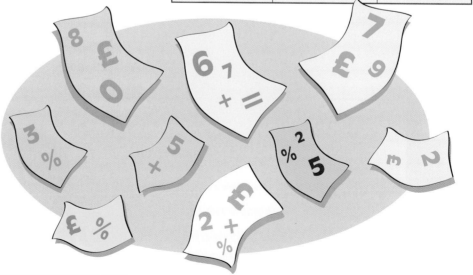

Q Why are performance ratios important?

B Different kinds of performance ratios

Ratio	What does it show?	Who might be interested?
Profitability		
Gross profit margin Gross profit : sales revenue $\dfrac{\text{Gross profit}}{\text{Sales revenue}} \times 100\%$	Gross profit for every £1 of sales. The bigger the %, the greater the profit.	Managers – is the firm performing well? Creditors – are profits enough to repay loans?
Net profit margin Net profit : sales revenue $\dfrac{\text{Net profit}}{\text{Sales revenue}} \times 100\%$	As before, but now allowing for fixed costs.	As before.
Return on capital employed (ROCE) Net profit : capital employed $\dfrac{\text{Net profit}}{\text{Capital employed}} \times 100\%$	Profit created from each £1 invested.	Shareholders (investors) – is investment providing as good a return as other options might?
Liquidity		
Current ratio Current assets : current liabilities	How easily a firm's short-term debts could be paid from current assets. Ratio of 1:1 means a firm is just covering its debts. Ratio of 3:1 means it has 3x the money needed to cover its debts. This is wasteful: the money could buy machinery, etc.	Managers, creditors – how easily can the firm's debts be covered? Linked to cash flow forecasts (see page 38).
Acid test ratio Current assets – stock: current liabilities	Current assets figures include stocks, which might be hard to turn into ready cash. Acid test, which removes them from the equation, is a more realistic measure. A reasonable figure is seen as between 0.5:1 and 1:1.	As before.

Remember
Some ratios are shown in figures, e.g. 1:3, others are written as %.

Q Which stakeholders would be interested in 'net profit margin'?

PRACTICE

Examine this extract from a balance sheet.

1 Calculate the company's current ratio.

> This should be written in the form A:B.

2 What does this ratio tell you about the success of the company?

Balance sheet as at 31.3.02

	£000	£000
Fixed assets		13 000
Current assets		
Stock	3880	
Debtors	40	
Cash	80	
	4000	
Current liabilities		
Creditors	720	
Overdraft	80	
	800	

People in business

➤ Managing people is vitally important: in a small business, managers have direct responsibility; in larger businesses, the Human Resource department assumes a part of this role.

A Managing people

KEY FACT

1 People are vital assets in a business and need to be managed effectively.

- The largest expenditure in most businesses is staff wages. Recruitment, training and the creation of good working relationships need careful management.

- In a small business, these responsibilities are usually held by the manager.

- In a large business, a Human Resource (HR) department is largely responsible for people management.

KEY FACT

2 HR departments carry out a wide range of tasks.

- These include: recruiting and training staff; preparing employment contracts, including legal requirements; dealing with negotiations between staff over pay and working conditions; supervising health and safety concerns.

Case study

A typical day for a Human Resources Manager at the head office of a computer retailer

1 Analyses results of a new bonus pay scheme. Sorts through job applications with the finance manager and arranges interviews.

2 Gives new sales staff employment contracts, shows them around and introduces them to their new colleagues.

3 Arranges a meeting with the despatch department to discuss a complaint over new teams.

4 Has a meeting with management and Union representatives to discuss teleworking from home for employees who work on the telephone all day.

During the day, deals with numerous phone calls, carries out a health and safety check on the office areas and spends time arranging the staff Christmas party.

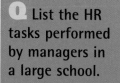
Q List the HR tasks performed by managers in a large school.

B Theories of motivation

Motivation theories offer explanations for human behaviour.

1 Maslow's Hierarchy of Needs

- Abraham Maslow analysed why people work. He drew a 'Hierarchy of Needs' pyramid from his findings.

- He ranked people's needs in order of importance, with the most basic at the bottom of the pyramid, and more advanced ones at the top.

- Maslow's theory suggests people won't be happy at work unless basic needs are met. For workers to stay motivated, they need to feel self-fulfilled, perhaps by being given responsibilities.

Self-fulfilment needs (reaching your potential)

Self-esteem needs (a sense of status)

Social needs (relationships with other workers)

Safety needs (job security, pension)

Basic needs / Survival (food and shelter or money to obtain these)

Remember
Maslow's needs can be learnt as the '5 Ss'.

2 Mayo's theory of job satisfaction

- Elton Mayo found that an employee's attitude was key.

- Increased personal satisfaction is the best form of motivation.

3 McGregor's theory X.Y

- Douglas McGregor studied managers' views of their employees. Two theories emerged:

  1) Theory X - workers don't like working, are just after money and need to be closely supervised.

  2) Theory Y - workers enjoy work, can be trusted, and can be motivated through job satisfaction.

- In McGregor's view, firms will be more successful if managers subscribe to theory Y.

Q As HR manager of a car company, how could you ensure your workers are satisfied in the short term and for the future?

PRACTICE

"The pay is poor, the hours long and I have to work at weekends."

"Everybody tells me what to do ... it is no fun."

1 What do these statements suggest about the motivation of hotel workers?

2 Identify and explain two possible ways in which workers' motivation could be improved.

> If your ideas draw on a motivation theory, mention the source.

Motivation and pay

THE BARE BONES

➤ Motivation means providing encouragement and incentives for workers.

➤ This can be achieved through different kinds of payment system.

A Financial and non-financial incentives

KEY FACT ➤

1 People have different reasons for working.

Motivation theories suggest these include:

- Earning money to survive and to pay for interesting activities.
- Providing social contact with other people.
- As a vocation, giving purpose to life.

KEY FACT

2 Incentives can be both financial and non-financial.

- Incentives affect people's commitment to work.
- Higher pay is an incentive to a person who works just for money, but it may also help motivate someone who is working for other reasons.

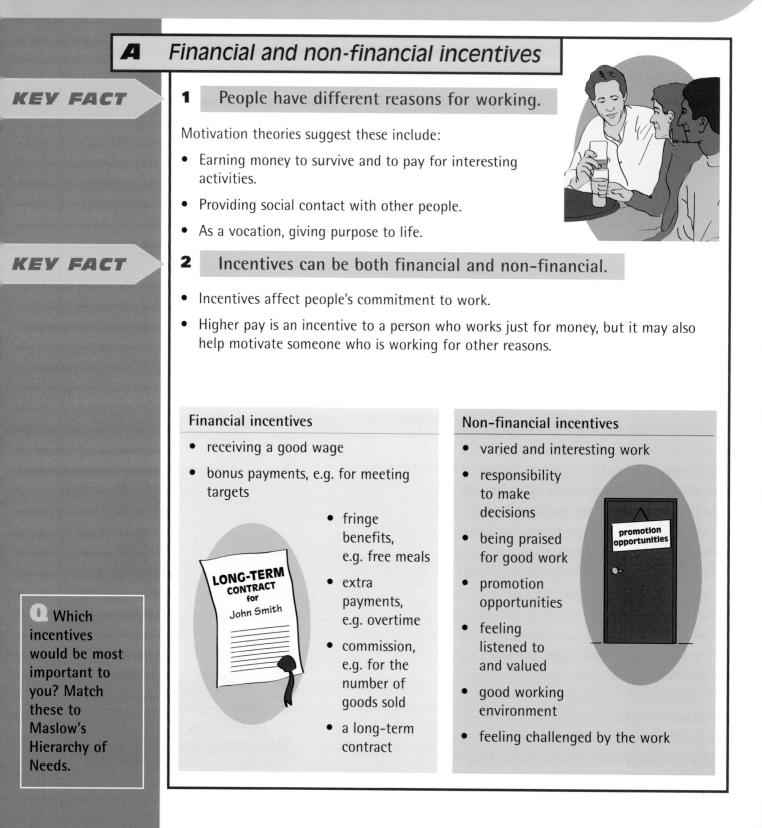

Financial incentives

- receiving a good wage
- bonus payments, e.g. for meeting targets
- fringe benefits, e.g. free meals
- extra payments, e.g. overtime
- commission, e.g. for the number of goods sold
- a long-term contract

LONG-TERM CONTRACT for John Smith

Non-financial incentives

- varied and interesting work
- responsibility to make decisions
- being praised for good work
- promotion opportunities
- feeling listened to and valued
- good working environment
- feeling challenged by the work

promotion opportunities

Q Which incentives would be most important to you? Match these to Maslow's Hierarchy of Needs.

B Motivation and pay

Different pay systems can influence the commitment of workers.

1 Wages and salaries - wages (most manual workers) are based on hourly rates, and are normally paid weekly. Salaries (most non-manual workers) are based on yearly figures, and paid directly into bank accounts each month. In both cases, income tax (PAYE in Britain) and National Insurance are deducted by the employer, and paid to the government. Some governments have set a national minimum (basic) wage.

2 Time rate - payment for the time taken to complete a job. Can encourage workers to take longer finishing a job to boost their pay.

3 Overtime - payment when a job cannot be completed in the normal time, often paid at a higher rate than normal.

4 Piece rate - payment for the number of products finished. Can encourage speed but may reduce quality.

5 Bonus payments - extra payments if a job is finished early or by a specified deadline.

6 Commission - payment of a (low) basic wage plus a percentage of the value of items sold or made. This is common practice in sales jobs.

7 Performance-related pay - another form of payment by results, where pay is linked to achievement of targets. Difficult to use in jobs where targets are not easily measured (e.g. nurses caring for different numbers of patients, with different levels of need).

8 Profit-sharing - extra payments based on company profit over a given period.

9 Fringe benefits - these include company cars, pensions, private healthcare, cheap loans. Managers are more likely to receive these than workers.

Remember
One payment system may not be the best for all the workers in a business.

Q What is the difference between overtime pay and bonus pay?

PRACTICE

Which type of payment and/or fringe benefits would be most suitable for the following workers? Give your reasons.

a) a cleaner

b) a salesperson

c) a nurse

d) a shop assistant

e) a lorry driver

Recruitment

THE BARE BONES
- ➤ The process of finding new staff must be well run to avoid wasting company time.
- ➤ Choosing the right person for a job largely depends on getting the right procedures and documents in place.

A The recruitment process

KEY FACT

1 An organisation must plan ahead to identify and fill job vacancies.

Vacancies arise for a variety of reasons, some planned and some unplanned. These include: retirement; promotion; the creation of new jobs through business expansion.

KEY FACT

2 The recruitment process can be seen as a set of separate stages.

The typical stages for a medium to large company are outlined below. A small company may not follow all of the procedures.

Remember
Job adverts and interviews must be fair and open to anyone with the right skills.

Step 1
The manager with the vacancy and the HR manager write a job description and person specification.

Step 2
A job advertisement is placed in a suitable publication. After the application deadline, CVs are checked to remove unsuitable applicants. The rest are compared to the person specification to arrive at a shortlist for interview.

Step 3
Candidates are interviewed, and may be given an appropriate test. The job is offered to the most suitable person (or readvertised if no candidate proves suitable). Unsuccessful candidates are notified.

Step 4
The successful candidate's references are checked. If any problems arise, the job may be offered to the next most suitable person from the list. If references are fine, a date is set for the new person to start.

Step 5
A contract and induction training are arranged. The performance of the new staff member is monitored via an appraisal system - manager and worker agree on targets for a set period, then review the results.

Q Which stages might a café manager use when appointing a new employee? What more informal methods might be used?

B Recruitment documents

Recruitment documents must be carefully written.

- Job descriptions are often used for years to identify the right skills, and to assess a person in their job.
- The wording must be accurate, fair and clear in its meaning.
- Candidates should take the same care writing applications or providing CVs.

The key contents of some recruitment documents are described below.

Job description:

drawn up by an employer. Lists all the duties the employee must carry out, as well as:

- the job title
- who they are responsible to
- who they are in charge of.

Job advertisement:

written by an employer. Contains details of a position to be filled, and where to apply. May be:

- internal - only circulated within the business to give existing staff the chance to apply
- external - advertised in local, national or specialist newspapers, Job Centres, recruitment agencies.

Person specification:

drawn up by an employer. Outlines the ideal candidate, and is used to find a person to fill the vacancy. Contains things like:

- qualifications required
- previous experience needed
- special skills needed, e.g. foreign languages
- personality needed, e.g. good telephone manner/confident nature for a receptionist.

CV (curriculum vitae):

written by a job applicant. Normally laid out like this:

- name
- date of birth
- address and telephone number
- educational qualifications
- previous jobs (starting with the most recent)
- interests
- names of referees (one is usually the last employer, or headteacher if the applicant is a school leaver).

Q What is the difference between a job description and a person specification?

PRACTICE

Explain the importance of a job description and an interview as part of the recruitment process.

It is helpful to refer to a particular job as an example.

Recruitment case study

THE BARE BONES

➤ This section demonstrates a type of exam question where you read and use material to answer questions.

➤ You must use relevant information from the case study in your answers.

Study all the information here, and use it to give full answers to the questions that follow.

Kim works for a computer company called Bytes, which sells from retail outlets and by mail order, and gives full after-sales support. She needs someone to work at the main warehouse, running the shop at the front and also giving advice and technical support to customers over the phone.

Kim and a colleague have drawn up the job description and person specification shown below. Having tried to recruit internally without success, she then placed an advertisement in the local paper. She has now narrowed down her shortlist to two candidates. Their CVs are shown opposite.

Job description

Title: Customer service representative

Responsible to: Sales manager
Responsible for: no staff

Function
- To sell hardware and software in the shop.
- To provide technical advice to customers.

Duties
- Start up demonstration machines in the shop each morning.
- Greet and assist customers.
- Demonstrate the use of the display machines and software.
- Operate the till and process cash and credit payments.
- Switch off all machines at the end of the day.
- Provide relief cover for telephone technical support staff when instructed.

Person specification

Position: Customer service representative

Educational qualifications

Essential: 5 GCSEs at grades A* - C to include either Business Studies or Computing

Desirable: A level or GNVQ Advanced in ICT

Experience: Previous retail experience preferred

Special skills: An interest in computers and good knowledge of current market for PCs and software

Personality: Polite, pleasant personality

Curriculum Vitae
PAULA TAIT

DATE OF BIRTH: 10th June 1984

10, High Street, Evesham

QUALIFICATIONS:

GCSE	English B
	French A
	Maths D
	Science C
	Business Studies C

EMPLOYMENT:

2000 to date: Sales Assistant, Woolworths, Evesham

INTERESTS:

Riding, walking

REFERENCES:

Headteacher, Courtmoor School, Evesham

Curriculum Vitae
KAREN LEWIS

DATE OF BIRTH: 29th May 1984

The Pines, Main Street, Evesham

QUALIFICATIONS:

GCSE	English	C
	Maths	C
	ICT	A
	Business Studies	B
	Art	C
GNVQ	Intermediate Business	merit

EMPLOYMENT:

To date 3 weeks work experience at a computer shop, plus Saturday work this year at the same shop.

INTERESTS: Music, computing

REFERENCES:

The Manager, Your PC, Evesham

PRACTICE

1 If you were Kim, which of the two candidates would you interview and why?

2 List six questions you would ask at interview.

3 What does the term recruit internally mean? What are the advantages of this?

> You need to identify the key requirements of the job, then decide who best meets these.

Training staff

THE BARE BONES

➤ Training is an important business activity which benefits both employers and employees.

➤ It can involve both new and experienced staff and take place on or off the job.

A Why training is important

KEY FACT

Training costs money but helps produce good quality staff and a good reputation for a business.

Remember
Training may cost money now but could benefit a business for years.

It is important for a variety of reasons:

1 An employer may have to buy expert guidance and pay staff while they train.

2 Unemployed people may have to develop their skills to help them get jobs.

3 People need training to cope with a new job.

4 Ongoing staff training is essential, as the business environment is constantly changing.

5 Workers need to acquire new skills and work flexibly.

6 Properly trained staff:
- are more productive and satisfied in their work
- take less time off and stay longer with a business, becoming experienced and highly skilled
- have confidence in their ability and are more likely to obtain promotion.

7 A business with a good training reputation is respected by staff, other employers and customers.

Q A supermarket installs new tills to help with stock control. Why would staff training benefit the employer and employees?

B Induction training

KEY FACT

Induction training helps new employees settle in to a business.

Induction training is given to new employees. It teaches them the basic skills required for the job, introduces them to the business and its expectations, may include a company presentation, e.g. a video, and can involve experienced employees acting as mentors to new recruits.

Case study

The first day at work

Karen receives a staff handbook on her first day. She is shown around and meets her new colleagues. She watches a video about the company and is shown how to use the display computers and the till.

Q What information/ guidance will Karen need on her first day at work?

C Training can take place on and off the job

Training can take place on the job or away from work.

1 On-the-job training: given while employees are working.

- May involve an employee being guided through a process.
- May also involve mentoring when an employee is teamed up with an experienced colleague (to discuss problems and progress).
- Skilled training staff may organise activities, e.g. group problem-solving tasks, role-playing.

2 Off-the-job training: specialist training which involves employees stopping their usual work.

- Often provided by another company at a training centre.
- Saves a business from having to employ its own training staff.
- Is useful when new technology requires specialist skills beyond the reach of a business.
- May be expensive to buy.
- Employees may be unwilling to travel/put up with the inconvenience.

Q What is the main difference between on-the-job training and off-the-job training?

D Government training schemes

Government schemes can improve workers' qualifications and help the unemployed back to work.

- Learning and Skills Councils manage training in regional areas. Grants are available for businesses promoting certain kinds of training, especially in IT.
- Investors in People (IIP) awards recognise quality training in businesses which set high standards, involve staff and evaluate their own success regularly.
- National Vocational Qualifications (NVQs) are awarded to people acquiring specific job skills, assessed in the workplace to set standards. Different levels of NVQ range from beginner to university-level.
- Modern apprenticeships are available for 16-25-year-olds to encourage vocational training at work.
- 'Welfare to work' government programme, aimed at younger people and long-term unemployed, will stop people claiming welfare benefits unless they join training programmes.

Q Name two government training schemes. Explain their benefits for employees and employers.

PRACTICE

Why might a company pay for off-the-job training to teach its employees to use new software?

You can explain the benefits for both the company and the employees.

Communication at work

A Internal and external communication

KEY FACT

Businesses need to communicate with staff internally and with customers and suppliers outside.

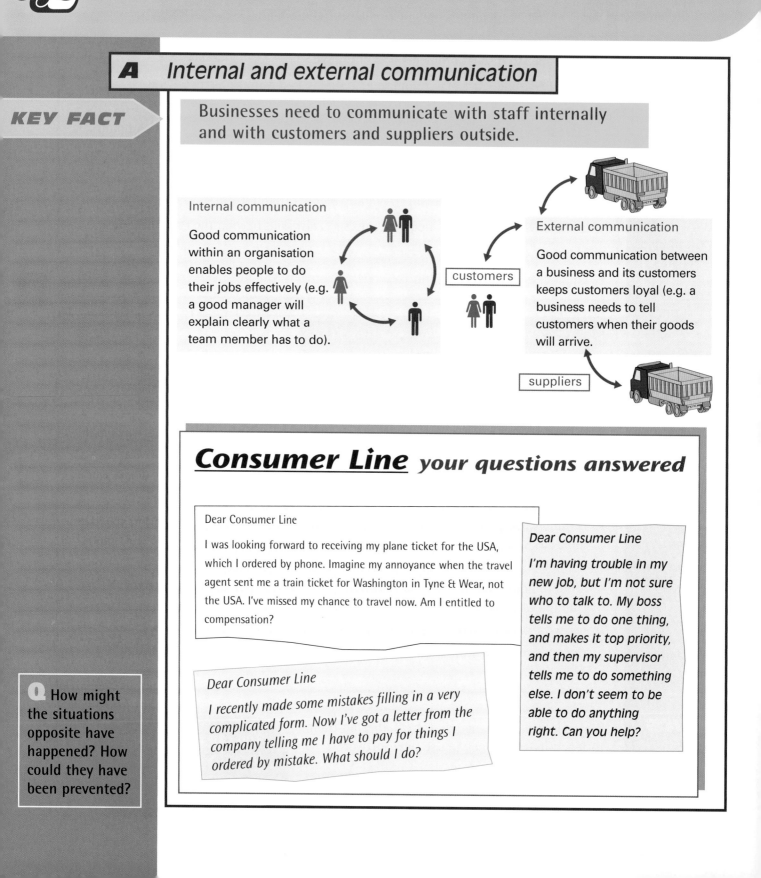

Internal communication

Good communication within an organisation enables people to do their jobs effectively (e.g. a good manager will explain clearly what a team member has to do).

customers

External communication

Good communication between a business and its customers keeps customers loyal (e.g. a business needs to tell customers when their goods will arrive.

suppliers

Consumer Line *your questions answered*

Dear Consumer Line

I was looking forward to receiving my plane ticket for the USA, which I ordered by phone. Imagine my annoyance when the travel agent sent me a train ticket for Washington in Tyne & Wear, not the USA. I've missed my chance to travel now. Am I entitled to compensation?

Dear Consumer Line

I'm having trouble in my new job, but I'm not sure who to talk to. My boss tells me to do one thing, and makes it top priority, and then my supervisor tells me to do something else. I don't seem to be able to do anything right. Can you help?

Dear Consumer Line

I recently made some mistakes filling in a very complicated form. Now I've got a letter from the company telling me I have to pay for things I ordered by mistake. What should I do?

Q How might the situations opposite have happened? How could they have been prevented?

B Channels of communication

1 The success of messages depends largely on organisation and choice of message type.

- The way a message is passed is called the channel of communication.

Written channels	Verbal channels
memo; letter; e-mail; fax; notice; report	meeting; telephone call; conversation; presentation; public address system
Written communications provide a permanent record on paper or disk.	Verbal communications provide speedy feedback and are especially good for negotiations.

2 A business needs to use the right kind of channel in the right direction.

Some channels fit their purpose and direction very well. For example:

- notices used as 'downwards' messages (from management to staff)
- reports used as 'upwards' messages (from staff to management)
- memos and e-mails used as 'sideways' messages (between colleagues).

C The importance of ICT

ICT has changed the way people work.

1 A personal computer with word processing, spreadsheets and databases allows a worker to write, process complex data and keep detailed records quickly and efficiently.

2 With a modem, information can be sent through the telephone network, giving e-mail facilities and access to the Internet.

3 Modems are also vital to teleworkers who usually work at home using computer technology to connect them to their employers. The employer can save on costs and employees can choose flexible working hours.

4 Suppliers and customers can contact businesses through websites on a worldwide basis.

Q When might a manager communicate with staff via:
a) memo;
b) formal report;
c) personal meeting?

Remember
Today, both speed and accuracy are required in most communications.

Q Name three ways in which ICT has changed workplace communication.

PRACTICE

What are the main advantages and disadvantages of teleworking for:
a) the employer?   b) the employee?

Industrial relations

➤ Good industrial relations are vital to modern workplaces.

➤ Trade unions/trade associations can help to represent workers and employers.

➤ The law provides a framework for good working conditions

A Good industrial relations

KEY FACT

1 In successful businesses, employers and workers respect each others' rights and decision making is fair.

- Industrial relations is the relationship between the workforce and the management of a business. Good relations mean difficult decisions are resolved openly and fairly.

- In any business, issues involving staff and management might be small (e.g. lateness), or more important and affect the whole workforce (e.g. pay negotiations).

- Businesses, especially large ones, need good organisation and a clear line of responsibility so that everyone knows what to do or who to talk to about problems.

KEY FACT

2 Employers and workers have different interests as well as shared concerns.

Everyone wants their business to be a success, but employers may be more concerned about cutting costs and selling products for profit. Workers may worry more about decent working conditions and a good pay packet. Both groups have to balance the protection of their own interests with their shared concern to meet customers' expectations.

Q What does being a 'good employer' mean in terms of industrial relations?

B Trade unions and trade associations

KEY FACT

Trade unions and trade associations represent workers and employers in discussions and disputes.

Trade unions look after the interests of the workers. Many people join a union because it will negotiate on their behalf, dealing with issues such as pay, holiday entitlement, redundancy and job security. Unions offer bargaining skills; services such as legal help in cases of unfair dismissal; advice on work-related matters; benefits such as cheaper insurance or personal loans.

Trade associations speak on behalf of employers. There are over 100 large associations and many smaller ones. Employers as a whole are represented by the CBI (Confederation of British Industry). They can negotiate pay; present the industry's view to the public; provide advice for firms.

Q What advantages might membership of a trade association offer to a small engineering company?

c Industrial relations, employment and the law

The law provides a framework for good working conditions.

- There have been many changes in the workplace in recent years. Few employers can offer a guaranteed job for life and many firms prefer to take workers as and when they need them.

- To ensure the fair treatment of all workers and responsible behaviour of all in the workplace, the government has created employment laws.

Things an employer must do	Things an employer must not do
Provide a written statement on pay, holidays and period of employment	Discriminate against workers on grounds of race, age, gender or disability (Equal Opportunities Laws)
Give equal pay to men and women if they are doing the same work	Stop a worker from belonging to a trade union
Give specific benefits to workers who have completed two years with the firm	Employ children under 13
Follow health and safety laws (Health and Safety at Work Act, 1974)	Dismiss a worker unfairly

Health and safety points to remember:

1 Employers must provide fire escapes, safety guards on machines and good toilets. Good overall hygiene standards should be kept.

2 Employers and employees should take reasonable care to look after their own and others' safety.

3 Employers must identify harmful tasks and minimise risks.

Equal opportunities points to remember:

1 Employers must show no discrimination on grounds of race, age, gender or disability in their:

2 selection procedures

3 contracts

4 training

5 benefits

6 selection for redundancy.

Remember
Many firms protect their workers with better policies than the law demands.

Remember
You don't need to know names and dates of employment laws but must know what is expected of firms.

Q Identify three ways in which the law protects workers in the workplace.

PRACTICE

Kimberly's paint factory pays well but workers have no protective clothing in the fume filled mixing section and no workers have written contracts. In what ways is this employer breaking the law and how could a trade union help the workers?

Negotiating

THE BARE BONES

➤ Most industries/businesses resolve issues (e.g. pay) by collective bargaining.

➤ Successful negotiations usually require compromise.

➤ Industrial action is difficult and costly but felt to be necessary at times.

A Collective bargaining

KEY FACT

Most industries and businesses decide pay and other issues by collective bargaining.

- Bargaining may be done at a national level, as with a nationwide industry, or at a local level with an individual business.

- Local negotiation may involve a small firm's union representative (sometimes called the shop steward) bargaining with management on behalf of company workers.

- Generally, different unions within a company will have their own representatives, who negotiate for their own workers.

- Some Far Eastern companies with factories in the UK have introduced new-style agreements with just one union to represent all workers.

- Some firms ask workers to sign no-strike agreements and put more emphasis on teamwork.

Q Why might a business prefer to have a single union to represent all its workers?

B Negotiation and compromise

KEY FACT

Successful negotiations between groups usually require some compromise.

Employers and workers need good working relationships. Where they disagree over issues like pay or conditions, the different groups put their case firmly but usually agree to give way on some issues in return for agreement on others.

Case study

Q What might everyone agree about? How might each group have to change its demands to reach agreement?

These workers and their employer are from a company making pre-packed cakes to sell to supermarkets. To stay in business, the cakes need to be made faster and at less cost. Talks on pay and machines are being held.

Employers want:
new machinery in to save costs
wages 2% up if workers also train to use machines
wages 2% up if more cakes are made

Skilled workers want:
a 10% pay rise to stay ahead of the others
new machines if they are the ones to use them

?

Unskilled workers:
want 7% pay rise
don't want to work with new machines

C Industrial action

If negotiations fail, more direct action can be taken.

1 Employers may close a factory. A union can call for industrial action to be taken. In either case, there are costs:

• Employers lose: production is stopped and customers may be lost.

• Workers lose: they won't be paid while on strike and may risk losing their jobs.

2 A union can call for its members to take industrial action, to try to pressurise management to accept the union's point of view. Unions must seek their members' opinions through a secret ballot (vote) before taking industrial action. Such action might involve a:

• strike (all workers stop work)

• ban on overtime

• boycott (of particular tasks)

• work to rule (only doing the tasks specified in your contract).

3 If agreement still can't be reached, the business might ask for help from ACAS (the Arbitration and Conciliation Advisory Service). They can provide independent people to conciliate (try to get the two sides to meet and discuss things) and arbitrate (decide what should be done).

Remember
There is no guarantee that arbitration will produce the result wanted by employers or by a union.

Q Name three different kinds of industrial action?

PRACTICE

1 How might a large firm making chocolate bars be affected by:
a) an overtime ban?
b) a work to rule by some workers?
c) an all-out strike?

2 Why might a 'single union agreement' be good for both employers and workers in a large firm?

Explain any assumptions behind your answer.

Choco Snacker

Business and marketing

THE BARE BONES
➤ In a competitive business world, a product needs to be marketed.
➤ A business needs to research information about its future prospects.

A   The importance of marketing

KEY FACT

In a competitive business world, a product needs to be marketed so consumers find out about it and buy it.

1 Businesses spend a significant part of their budget on marketing, so getting it right is important.

2 Marketing activities involve:
- finding out about consumer tastes and opinions
- providing the right products in the right place at the right time
- promoting the products to inform and persuade consumers to buy.

3 Marketing has limits: no amount of packaging will sell a poor product longer term.

4 Laws prevent a business making false claims about its products.

Remember
A well-designed product may not sell well if marketing is poor.

Key features of marketing		Example: marketing a children's video
Most firms are **market-orientated**: they aim to make what consumers want at a price that sells and makes profit. **Market research** ensures the product suits the market.		Children's video makers know new products must look good, be affordable, and have a new theme/characters to appeal to the age group.
Consumers can be classified into groups or **market segments**. Advertising campaigns and pricing can be targeted at the group most likely to buy the product.		A video will be wanted by children, but bought by parents, so may advertise in comics and on kids' TV and run high street poster campaigns.
Clever **promotion** can extend the sales of a product for long periods. **Attractive packaging**, links with popular places or celebrities and spin-off products are all techniques which can extend a product's life cycle.		The packaging of a free toy character with a children's video, for instance, or special repackaging of the video for Christmas, will keep the original product in the public eye.
Price is a key factor in maximising market share. A business must make the correct pricing decisions to cover costs, make a profit and compete with rivals. Special deals/different price bands may prove useful.		£7.99 sounds much cheaper than just 1p off £8.00

Q Managers of a leisure centre want more customers. How could they classify the centre's users to send out adverts and set appropriate prices?

B Researching past and future performance

1 A business uses existing data to check past performance and research questions to find future trends.

Information on past performance:
- are sales up or down on last year?
- has our market share increased?
- have our profits increased?
- why did this product fail?
- which products did best?

Information on current status:
- how much market share do we have?
- who is buying our products?
- why are they buying them?
- are our prices competitive?
- is advertising reaching the right people?
- are customers satisfied with quality?
- is someone else's product selling better?
- which of our products are selling best?

Information on future trends:
- can we keep sales going on existing products?
- can we launch a new product?
- which groups should we aim it at?
- what share of the market can we expect to win?
- are competitors planning new products?
- are there any new competitors?
- are there any new laws or technologies to consider?

2 SWOT analysis helps a business examine its strengths and weaknesses.

SWOT analysis can be used to look at market position and how this could be improved. It reminds a business that its strengths may lie in, for example, the way it is organised or is managing costs. It could have advantages over rivals but these may not last.

Strengths and Weaknesses	Internal factors over which a business has some control, e.g. costs of overheads, materials and labour	Ford (UK) produces a good range of family cars Unit costs are high in the UK
Opportunities and Threats	External factors over which a business has little or no control, e.g. the performance of a competitor, new government legislation	Rover is struggling as a business and has been taken over by a European rival The government is looking to see if UK companies are setting car prices too high

Q What are the benefits to a business of using SWOT analysis?

PRACTICE

Mobile phones produced by a large European company are not selling as well as they were. What information should the company research to help it decide on its future?

Use the SWOT framework to organise your answer.

Market research

THE BARE BONES
➤ Businesses classify their customers for research purposes.
➤ Research involves analysing primary or secondary data.
➤ Surveys can provide quantitative or qualitative data.

A Market segments

Businesses divide customers into groups (market segments), according to different characteristics.

A business may want to know which sex or age group is particularly keen on a product. This gives them a target audience for their advertising, and helps in refining the product.

1 Socio-economic market segments, used by government and many businesses, are based on characteristics of income, education and occupation:

Group A	Professionals	3%	Group C2	Skilled manual	33%
Group B	Management/technical	12%	Group D	Semi-skilled manual	20%
Group C1	Supervisory/clerical	22%	Group E	Unskilled manual	10%

2 Focus groups bring together typical customers of a particular product to find their opinions about the product. They can be based on gender, age, race or lifestyle and are used increasingly by businesses.

Q What is meant by the term market segments?

B Desk and field research

Research involves collecting and analysing information. It can be expensive and time-consuming.

- **Field research**: collecting and analysing information gained first-hand, via interviews or surveys (primary data).

- **Desk research**: working with existing material, e.g. rivals' published accounts (secondary data).

Remember
The speed at which a business can obtain information is important.

Q Identify three key differences between primary and secondary data.

Primary data (original)
Up-to-date, directly relevant to products.
Targeted at customers of a business.
Remains confidential to a business.
Can be expensive.

Secondary data (published)
Wide range of general data available.
Quick to handle.
Usually free.
Can be out-of-date or off-target.

C *Different kinds of surveys, questions and results*

When deciding which type of survey to use, quantity of response must be weighed against quality.

1 Types of survey

- One-on-one surveys: usually street or telephone questionnaires (good for quantity of data) or longer in-depth interviews (good for quality).

- Postal surveys: easy to set up, but usually low response rates and low quality of data.

- Group surveys: people meet to discuss a product (high quality, low quantity data).

- Random survey: each person (in a given area) has an equal chance of selection.

- Survey based on quotas: a set number of people from each market segment are interviewed.

- Targeted surveys: questions are put to one particular market segment.

2 Types of question

- Closed: the interviewee chooses from a set of possible answers, e.g. multiple choice questions or scales. Answers are easy to analyse, but provide limited data.

- Open: no pre-set answers. Answers can be more valuable but are harder to analyse.

3 Results

- Quantitative information is easily presented as graphs or charts, e.g. to show which groups are buying a product most.

- Qualitative information gives detail and depth, and data is often presented as examples or case studies, e.g. to explain why a product appeals to a particular group.

Q Name three kinds of survey used by businesses to gather data.

PRACTICE

A petrol station is planning to expand its payment area to include a small shop, offering a range of services and products.

1 The petrol station manager wants to know the age range and occupation of the customers. List two other pieces of data about the customers that would be useful.

2 Explain why this sort of data is useful.

THE BARE BONES

➤ The marketing mix is the ingredients that businesses use to achieve marketing aims.

➤ A business may change its marketing strategy over time by altering its marketing mix.

A   The 'four Ps' of the marketing mix

KEY FACT

The marketing mix is made up of Product, Promotion, Price and Place.

A successful marketing mix of a good product in the right place at the right price, with attractive packaging and advertising, wins customers and makes profits more likely. Decisions have to be made about:

Remember
Companies place different emphasis on elements of the marketing mix.

Product
● Quality: needs constant review.
● Range: develop new products, or concentrate on small number?
● After sales service: builds reputations and sales.
● Features and facilities: alterations/updates can completely 'remake' a product.
● Size and packaging: may be crucial to customers.

Promotion
● Expenditure: how much?
● Style and substance: posters, adverts, local leafleting?
● Timing: regular, seasonal, aimed at particular time of day? Vital at launch of new product.
● Media: press, TV, point-of-sale, telephone, local or national?

The four Ps

Price
● Basic price level: needs constant review.
● Discounts: could win new customers.
● Pricing: varies for different customers.

Place
● Distribution: most common distribution chain is producer-wholesaler-retailer-customer, but shorter chains, e.g. producer-consumer, cut costs.
● Direct selling: home selling, mail order, TV and computer sales are all growing sectors of the market.
● Delivery and stock levels: sales lost if these areas are inefficient. Increase delivery fleet?

Q Explain the marketing mix of a company advertising on peak-time TV a big hits, low price CD only available by mail order.

B   The marketing strategy and marketing mix

In creating the marketing mix for a product, a business will concentrate on different elements from the lists opposite: the business has an underlying strategy which depends on factors such as whether the product is new or the market highly competitive.

1 If the marketing strategy is to establish, with a limited budget, a new product in an existing market, a company might decide to concentrate on low pricing or on swift and efficient delivery or it may rely instead on word-of-mouth marketing.

2 If a business is trying to boost the sales of a well-established product, it may create new product features, improve the product quality, run a new advertising campaign or try to attract a new group of customers.

New technology has made a big difference to the marketing strategies of some businesses e.g. bookshops. Internet sites allow access to customers worldwide. A marketing campaign to promote the website address, then a well-designed website backed by good customer service, should increase sales.

Q Identify three ways in which a business could improve the sales of a well-known washing powder.

PRACTICE

A fast food chain is opening a new restaurant in a town centre. Marketing efforts will be aimed at raising awareness among local people. Future marketing will depend on the sales revenue from the restaurant. The budget is £10 000, and various methods could be used:

Large posters on key sites	£400 per poster per month
Local leaflets	£175 per 10 000 leaflets
Local newspaper adverts	£550 per advert
Local schools competition	£500 for prizes
Meal discount offers	£2 per meal
Radio adverts	£300 per 30 seconds

1 What methods would you use to promote the fast food restaurant and why?

2 Once the restaurant was open, what marketing mix could be used to ensure customers kept returning?

You don't need to write about all the 'four Ps' in every answer. Choose only those most relevant to the situation.

The product life cycle

THE BARE BONES
➤ Products have a natural life cycle which can be shown on a graph.
➤ Businesses use many methods to try to extend product life cycles.
➤ Branding is important to establish a particular product.

A The product life cycle

KEY FACT

1 Products have a natural life cycle.

A product's life cycle begins with its development and launch, moves through a period of growth to maturity, then reaches a point where the market is full of similar competing products. Finally a loss of sales leads to the end of the cycle.

KEY FACT

2 Forward-looking businesses constantly try to develop new and improved products.

• Product development may take a long time and be costly, especially where health and safety are important product features.

• The main elements in product development are: establishing customer needs; generating new ideas; checking production is viable and that the business can afford to go ahead; producing and testing prototypes; test marketing; developing a marketing strategy.

KEY FACT

3 The stages of a product life cycle can be shown on a graph.

Remember
The graph shape will vary according to the product and length of its cycle.

Q What is the main difference between the life cycle of a computer game and a product like salt?

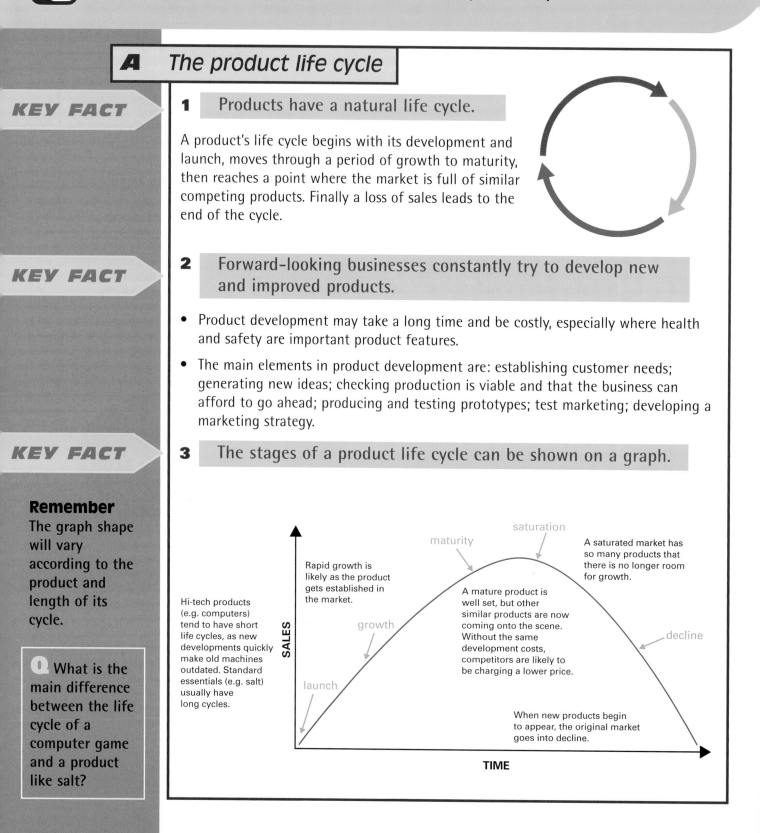

Hi-tech products (e.g. computers) tend to have short life cycles, as new developments quickly make old machines outdated. Standard essentials (e.g. salt) usually have long cycles.

Rapid growth is likely as the product gets established in the market.

A mature product is well set, but other similar products are now coming onto the scene. Without the same development costs, competitors are likely to be charging a lower price.

A saturated market has so many products that there is no longer room for growth.

When new products begin to appear, the original market goes into decline.

launch · growth · maturity · saturation · decline

SALES / TIME

B Extending the life cycle

Businesses use many methods to try to extend product life cycles.

1 However brilliant, a product unwanted by consumers will not sell. Other products may sell well for a while, then lose popularity. Firms spend lots of money on research and development before marketing a product, and on extending a product's life cycle once it is in the market.

2 Life cycles can be lengthened by: extra advertising/promotion; new packaging (e.g. luxury versions); special deals; widening the product range (e.g. making videos of books); changing the product image to aim at a new market segment; diversifying a product (e.g. Mars ice cream bar).

Q How could the life cycle of a mobile phone be extended?

Branding

1 Branding involves developing a product's name with a logo, colours and packaging, and registering it to stop other companies from using it.

2 Branding helps preserve the life of a product by: making customers feel secure regarding quality; making it hard for new rivals to gain attention; making it simpler for customers to choose.

3 **Strong branding is evident in the sweets market** with some £126 million spent each year on advertising. A new brand can be a 'top twenty' selling sweet within a year or two, but big firms like Cadbury's have successfully maintained up to forty brand versions of chocolate.

4 Many **high-street stores and supermarkets have copied the idea** of branding for their own range of products. **'Own brands'** now account for one-third of sales in supermarkets.

5 **Branding may not work where products are seen as essentially the same** by consumers. Fresh fruit is an example, although Outspan and others have had some success.

6 A market leader's name is often used to refer to all products in the market (e.g. biros, hoovers).

Remember
Fashions can repeat themselves. Yoyos have come back to life after decline on several occasions.

Q What are the advantages to a business of a good brand name?

PRACTICE

Allsports manufactures high quality sports and leisure shoes for specialist shops and department stores to sell under their own labels. It is now thinking of marketing its own brand label of sports shoes in this very competitive market.

1 What is meant by a 'very competitive market'? Use examples to illustrate your answer.

2 What problems might Allsports have in marketing its own brand label?

Pricing decisions

THE BARE BONES

➤ The price of a product is determined by supply (from producers) and demand (of consumers).

➤ Businesses use different pricing policies to win or hold market share.

A Price, supply and demand

Remember
A supply and demand diagram helps predict what will happen if demand is greater/less than supply.

The price that satisfies both business and customers will 'clear' the market.

In theory:

1 The higher the price of a product, the more a business will supply.

2 The higher the price, the less consumers will demand.

3 The ideal price is where supply and demand meet (the equilibrium price).

4 The equilibrium price satisfies both a business and its customers and the market will 'clear'.

5 Too low a price, and demand will outstrip supply. Too high a price, and there will be a surplus of unsold products.

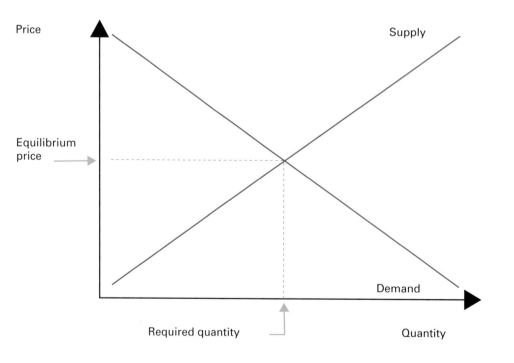

Q Tickets for a concert cost £20 and the hall is half full. Draw a supply and demand diagram to show this. What price might fill the hall?

In practice, it is difficult to get information about all the decisions of businesses and consumers, so businesses set prices based on their objectives and 'best guesses' about the state of the market.

B Pricing policies

Pricing is part of an overall marketing strategy used to persuade customers to buy a product.

Prices must be monitored and adjusted when necessary to take account of such things as new competition, or rises and falls in demand.

1 Cost-plus pricing: a percentage mark-up is added to the total unit costs of production to give a business its profit margin. This takes no account of variations in fixed costs with output, or what customers will pay, but is a common approach. (A similar policy, contribution pricing, sets prices to cover variable costs and make a contribution towards fixed costs.)

2 Competitive pricing: a firm sets its price close to those of its rivals so competition effectively focuses on non-price features such as quality of service.

3 Loss-leaders: prices are set at or below cost in order to penetrate a new market. Supermarkets often use this approach, attracting customers to cheap goods on the basis that they will then buy other items. Penetration pricing is similar, with prices set above cost but below rivals.

4 Skimming (or creaming) the market: highlights a product's uniqueness, e.g. new hi-tech equipment is often given a high price as some people will buy it as a luxury. This enables development costs to be recovered. Later, the price can be dropped to attract a wider market.

5 Price discrimination: different prices are charged to different groups for the same product. Rail companies and airlines use this widely, e.g. some train passengers are charged a premium for rush hour travel while others can fill empty seats at a low price during off-peak times.

student with railcard | last minute one-day saver | pre-booked first-class season ticket | family ticket

6 Consumer-led pricing: consumers develop a sense of a 'fair price', and products priced too far above or below this won't sell well, unless seen as true 'luxury' or 'bargain' products. This is known as a 'price plateau' and all businesses must be aware of it.

Remember
Pricing can be a matter of psychology. £2.00 is not a good price; £1.99 'feels' much lower.

Q What is the difference between competitive pricing and price-skimming?

PRACTICE

Fill-up Foods plc make and sell snacks in a very competitive market. Research suggests a gap in the adult snacks market, but pricing will be vital.
The marketing manager suggests prices should start low and then rise once brand loyalty is established.

1 Explain what might happen to sales if Fill-up's price was higher than its competitors.

2 Suggest and explain alternative pricing policies that the company might use.

Think about how the company can gain an edge over its rivals. Pricing policies will differ according to the level of competition.

Promoting products

➤ Promotion is how a firm tells likely customers about a product and its benefits, in order to boost sales.

➤ It involves a mixture of information and persuasion and includes everything from advertising to free gifts.

A Promotion

KEY FACT

Promotion involves the way a product and its strengths are presented to consumers.

- As part of its marketing strategy, a business may choose to spend more or less money on the promotion of a product at different stages in its life cycle.

- A promotion campaign may be targeted at a national audience using every method available or may be a more local direct mail shot on a relatively small budget. It can set out to inform customers about the special features of a new product or try to persuade them that a product is better than others.

Q What is 'promotion'? Give three examples of recent promotional campaigns for products.

B Advertising

KEY FACT

Advertising is an important way of promoting a product.

Remember
The Advertising Standards Authority controls bad advertising.

1 Most companies use some form of advertising to promote their products. This can be through a variety of media, such as: TV, radio and cinema; newspapers and magazines; journals or specialist publications; posters on billboards.

Q What are the pros and cons of advertising during a top-rated TV show?

2 Some types of advertising are more expensive than others, and are likely to reach many more people. Businesses spend over £10 billion on advertising in the UK. The largest part is spent on press and TV adverts.

3 Companies advertise: to persuade people to buy the product; to change people's attitudes; to make people think better of an organisation; to provide basic information.

c Other types of promotion

Other forms of promotion can be short term (e.g. a one-off direct mailing) or part of a longer-term activity (e.g. a three-year sports sponsorship deal).

Public relations activities aim to keep a company's name in the public eye and ensure good customer relations. A public relations department is responsible for:

- press releases (e.g. about a new product)
- organising sponsorships and awards (e.g. for sports or educational activities)
- damage limitation - putting the company point of view in the event of unfavourable publicity.

Sales promotion activities include:

- special offers (buy two, get one free)
- price discounts
- vouchers, coupons and customer loyalty cards
- joint promotions (where one firm links to another, e.g. McDonald's and Disney)
- point of sale materials (displays and packaging in store)
- free gift campaigns or prize competitions (e.g. in children's book or toy shops).

Direct mailing ('junk mail'):

- involves sending promotional material to targeted customers
- uses databases of names built up from questionnaires, guarantee cards etc.
- is used to promote a variety of goods and services (e.g. book and music clubs, financial services, charity work).

Packaging often defines and identifies a product, and can be the most persuasive ingredient when consumers choose an item from the shelf:

- Good packaging must protect the product.
- It must be the right size and shape for easy use by distributors and customers.
- It must also have consumer appeal.
- Many large companies use professional design agencies to help them develop the most eye-catching look, and also to create seasonal looks, e.g. at Christmas.

Q Identify one short-term and one long-term promotional activity.

PRACTICE

Fill-up Foods plc hopes to sell more snacks in pubs, supermarkets and garages. What are the pros and cons of running a local TV advertising campaign to promote a new snack?

Remember the pros and cons are with reference to other means of promotion.

The business environment

THE BARE BONES

➤ The success of a business partly depends on external factors.
➤ Businesses face many risks and must plan for uncertainties as well as foreseeable events.

A   External influences

KEY FACT

A business's success depends on external as well as internal influences.

Business rivals

can be a threat if their prices are lower

can help to boost trade for everyone

prices and quality to compete with

Industry

may set guidelines, e.g. on pollution

may promote products for all businesses

voluntary codes to abide by

Government

legislation may affect business costs

can help to raise business confidence

laws to abide by, agencies to satisfy

Business

demands for choice and quality to fulfil

demands for good practice

overseas markets more accessible via the Internet

consumer tastes may change

can stay loyal to a particular brand

Customers

can be a threat if they gain publicity

can be a boost if products seen to be good

Pressure groups

ups and downs in trade

a slump in a big economy can affect everyone

Global economy

Q List three external factors which may influence a global oil company with a bad reputation for pollution.

B Planning for uncertainty

The external business environment is full of risks.
Good planning and government support can minimise these risks.

A number of external factors can create difficulties for a business. For instance:

- If the economic outlook is gloomy, a new business or product will be less likely to succeed.
- An unforeseen problem with a product may be discovered.
- Rival firms may use new technology to improve their products.
- Interest rates may rise, increasing the cost of loans.
- Exchange rates may change, making foreign trade more difficult.

Facing up to uncertainty and change

If just one store sold computers, it could set a high price. When many businesses are competing, expect lower prices, better service and lots of new products. **A business can monitor rivals when planning new products/marketing campaigns.**

Large out-of-town stores offer choice and cheaper prices to customers with cars and can benefit local communities. But there may be costs - town centre shops can lose customers and traffic may increase. **Government planning rules can help balance the interests of communities, small local businesses and big stores.**

Computer sales rely on good marketing and customers having money to spend. If unemployment rises and people cut back on spending, selling products will be more difficult. High interest rates make it hard for businesses to borrow funds for investment/product development. **The government's bank can help by managing interest rates. Businesses need to time any big loans carefully.**

A UK computer software business selling to the home market is likely to face competition from foreign firms. The business may also wish to sell abroad. Its prices may be lower than its rivals but a high UK exchange rate can make it hard to sell to other countries. Labour costs may be lower in other countries and a UK business may find it hard to compete. **The business may use new technology to keep costs down. Governments can help by managing exchange rates.**

Q Name three external difficulties which can face a business.

PRACTICE

Identify three ways in which a government could help business activity in the UK.

Use different examples of government support rather than similar schemes.

Business and competition

➤ Competition is usually good for businesses and customers but can lead to bad practices.

➤ There are laws to protect businesses and consumers.

A The importance of business competition

KEY FACT

To survive in a competitive industry, a business must win customers by meeting their needs.

1 Competition creates **choice for consumers** and ensures businesses minimise costs and invest in developing new products. Businesses that cut corners to win customers may gain a bad reputation.

2 Businesses generally operate in **competitive environments**, for instance: where there are many rivals (e.g. town centre clothes shops); where customers have a wide choice of products (e.g. restaurants).

3 A business will generally do well if it: gives good personal service and is known to replace faulty products; has good marketing techniques; has competitive pricing; provides high levels of quality and standards; responds well to issues raised by pressure groups.

Q Why might a successful restaurant welcome a new rival opening nearby?

B Why businesses need controls

KEY FACT

Competition may lead to businesses behaving in unacceptable ways.

1 Businesses can exaggerate claims for their products.

2 Successful firms may charge very low prices to force rivals out of business.

3 When one firm dominates a market they may disregard customer views.

4 Some products may be profitable but undesirable (e.g. cigarettes, alcohol).

Q Why does the government set rules for business advertising?

C Controls on businesses

KEY FACT

Business competition is regulated through various mechanisms.

Competition laws

UK and European Union laws stop businesses fixing prices or restricting supply. In Britain, the Competition Commission investigates cases where:

• 25% or more of the market is in one business's hands

• a merger between businesses involves assets over £70 million.

Remember
Competition helps keep down costs but can lead to wasteful advertising.

C Consumer laws

The three main laws protecting the consumer are:

1 Trade Descriptions Act (1968, 1972): Stops firms giving misleading information.

2 Consumer Credit Act 1974: Protection when borrowing or buying on credit.

3 Sale and Supply of Goods Act 1994: Products have to be of 'satisfactory quality'.

Local government organisations

- Trading Standards Officers check on faulty products and weights and measures.
- Environmental Health Officers check on issues such as food hygiene and pollution.
- An Ombudsman checks public complaints, e.g. against government services.

Independent organisations

- The British Standards Institute (BSI) tests products for safety and quality and issues 'Kitemarks' to products that meet certain standards.
- Citizens Advice Bureaux provide free advice and help people to make complaints.
- The Office of Fair Trading provides information and advice leaflets.
- Agencies set up by the Government, e.g. OFTEL, OFGAS, check that private businesses don't abuse their monopoly position.

Voluntary codes

- Some industries have their own codes of conduct, e.g. the Association of British Travel Agents (ABTA) promises to get customers home from holiday if a firm goes bust.
- The Advertising Standards Authority (ASA) encourages advertisers to make 'legal, decent, honest and truthful' adverts.

Q Name three ways in which consumers are protected from dishonest businesses.

PRACTICE

Baz reduces the price of some T-shirts in his shop. He labels each one to say it has faded after being on display. A customer buys one but returns it the next day demanding her money back.

1 Is the customer's complaint justified? Refer to relevant consumer protection laws.

2 State and explain one action Baz could take.

3 Suggest two organisations where the consumer could get advice.

4 What actions could these organisations take if the law had been broken?

Learn the main two or three consumer protection laws and the key reason for each one.

Business and the community

THE BARE BONES

➤ Businesses need good working relationships with their local community to operate successfully.

➤ Some costs and benefits of business activities may be felt by the wider community.

A Businesses need the goodwill of a local community

KEY FACT

A business needs the goodwill of a local community to survive long term.

A business may feel its main interest is in making a profit and that local community interests are not a priority. But a business needs:

1 planning consent to operate in a community - planning laws may be used against unpopular businesses

2 transport facilities and other services provided at a cost by the local community

3 employees and possibly emergency support from the local area.

Q What is meant by the 'goodwill of the community'?

B External costs and benefits

KEY FACT

Business activity has costs and benefits which are included in prices and profits. Other external costs and benefits felt by the community are not taken into account by individual firms.

External benefits add to the welfare of the community, but external costs cause problems. It can be difficult to get anyone to take responsibility for damage and hard to put a figure on the cost.

To have a medium-sized business set up or expand in an area:

External benefits may include:
✓ Improved transport and communications; job gains (new employment and income); extra spending in local shops from those employed; regeneration of local area (new buildings, shops etc. because of new wealth); efficient recycling (some businesses use heat from waste burners as a power source).

External costs may include:
✗ Pollution; safety hazards from factories and traffic; waste products for disposal (general rubbish, smoke, gases, toxic substances); building in rural areas (damage to beauty spots and wildlife populations); job losses (unemployment from failure and closure of rival businesses); lost income and spending power of those unemployed; loss of local services (useful local buildings/services may be closed to make way for developments).

B

A proposal for an out-of-town shopping centre might attract support from those who consider more shops, jobs and a better image for the town as being of great benefit to the local community.

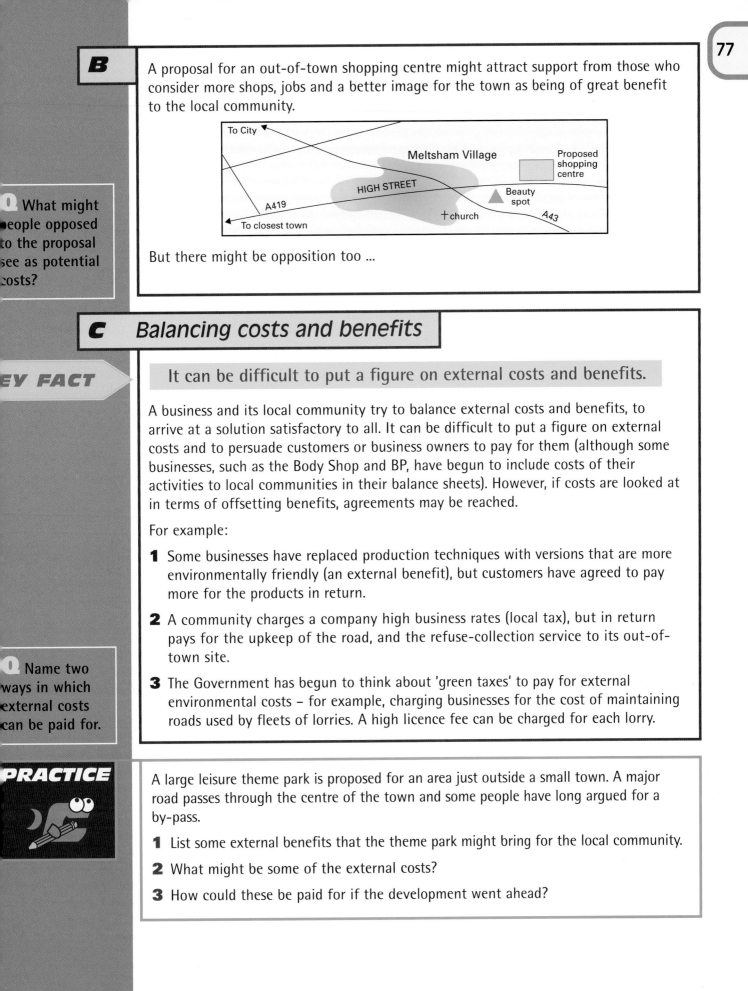

Meltsham Village

Proposed shopping centre

To City

HIGH STREET

A419

To closest town

Beauty spot

+ church

A43

But there might be opposition too ...

Q What might people opposed to the proposal see as potential costs?

C *Balancing costs and benefits*

> It can be difficult to put a figure on external costs and benefits.

A business and its local community try to balance external costs and benefits, to arrive at a solution satisfactory to all. It can be difficult to put a figure on external costs and to persuade customers or business owners to pay for them (although some businesses, such as the Body Shop and BP, have begun to include costs of their activities to local communities in their balance sheets). However, if costs are looked at in terms of offsetting benefits, agreements may be reached.

For example:

1 Some businesses have replaced production techniques with versions that are more environmentally friendly (an external benefit), but customers have agreed to pay more for the products in return.

2 A community charges a company high business rates (local tax), but in return pays for the upkeep of the road, and the refuse-collection service to its out-of-town site.

3 The Government has begun to think about 'green taxes' to pay for external environmental costs – for example, charging businesses for the cost of maintaining roads used by fleets of lorries. A high licence fee can be charged for each lorry.

Q Name two ways in which external costs can be paid for.

PRACTICE

A large leisure theme park is proposed for an area just outside a small town. A major road passes through the centre of the town and some people have long argued for a by-pass.

1 List some external benefits that the theme park might bring for the local community.

2 What might be some of the external costs?

3 How could these be paid for if the development went ahead?

The national economy

THE BARE BONES
➤ Governments try to manage the economy to provide stability for businesses.
➤ They raise taxes to pay for different policies.

A How governments manage the economy

KEY FACT

Governments manage the economy to provide stability for businesses.

Business activity can be affected by government policies and the state of the national economy. Businesses expect governments to steer the economy towards steady growth and avoid sharp fluctuations in prices, interest rates and exchange rates.

In the UK, we also expect our government to: provide some goods and services for everyone; ensure the poorest are helped by the better-off (through taxes and benefits); keep price levels steady and encourage training and jobs.

The government uses different policies to affect the economy:

1 It taxes income, spending and business profits then uses the money for welfare benefits, services (e.g. health, education) and investment in new roads/buildings. Some of these policies are targeted at poorer regions of the country.

2 Tax and spending (fiscal policy) is managed through the yearly Budget.

3 The government's bank makes changes in interest rates (monetary policy) to encourage borrowing and investment by consumers and businesses.

Q Identify three ways in which the government is expected to manage the economy.

B Managing the business cycle

KEY FACT

The government tries to smooth out big swings in the business cycle.

Remember
Governments can help but can't control all the factors that make business risky.

Q What could a government do to help businesses if unemployment is rising and the outlook is gloomy?

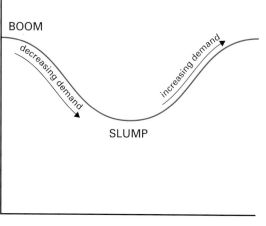

Growth in UK business output averages 2-3% a year but tends to fluctuate in cycles every 4-5 years. Growth and employment are helped by high demand in the economy. If demand outstrips supply, there can be a general increase in prices (inflation) and business planning becomes difficult.
If the government raises taxes, it can reduce demand but at the risk of pushing up unemployment and shaking business confidence.

B

Rising prices affect:

Jobs: fewer goods bought by consumers, falling sales, cut back on employment.

Trade: UK goods prices rise faster than those of foreign competitors; exports fall, imports rise.

Business costs: prices of raw materials rise; workers want more pay to cover higher prices; upward pressure on business costs.

C How a government raises and uses taxes

EY FACT

Governments raise taxes in various ways from individuals and businesses to pay for different policies.

Income tax: the UK government takes 30-35% of pay through income tax and national insurance contributions. Currently, the basic rate of income tax is 20% for most workers. A higher rate leaves people with less income so discourages spending.

Value Added Tax (VAT): a tax on spending (17.5% on most goods and services; excludes essentials like children's clothes and basic food). A higher rate may discourage spending and push up prices.

Corporation tax: paid by companies on their income (profit). A rise in this tax could mean less investment and so cut future employment levels.

What does the government do with the money taken in taxes?

The money pays for education, health and other services as well as a wide range of welfare benefits. It also helps businesses through a variety of schemes:

1 Assisted areas: grants given to businesses who set up within a designated area.

2 Inner cities: development corporations take over a whole area that has declined, rebuild the infrastructure and oversee private sector investment in the area.

3 Enterprise zones: business spending on new buildings is not taxed in these areas and businesses do not have to pay business rates for a period of time.

4 Small businesses: given help with loans and start-ups.

The European Union also provides grants and has Enterprise Zone schemes.

Q What is the difference between income tax and value added tax?

PRACTICE

A Canadian Company, Carco, wants to open a factory in Kirston, a UK town in decline since the closure of a major industrial plant. The local council has worked hard to improve roads and subsidise a new industrial estate, which has been designated as an Enterprise Zone.

1 Kirston Business Park is an Enterprise Zone. What does this mean to Carco?

2 How else will Carco benefit from setting up in Kirston?

3 Why is the arrival of Carco important for the region and for the economy?

Avoid phrases like 'they can do this' when writing about government activity. Be specific: refer to the government or local councils as appropriate.

THE BARE BONES

> ➤ The European Union (EU) provides a common trading area for 25 countries.
> ➤ The Euro is a common currency used by most EU members, but not currently the UK.

A The EU as a common trading area

KEY FACT

> The EU provides a common trading area which offers many shared benefits.

1 UK businesses operate in a combined EU market of some 370 million people.

2 The EU has regulations, policies and guidelines which help and control business activity.

3 Over 58% of the UK's overseas trade is with other EU countries.

4 The EU aims to achieve social and economic progress for its members through economic growth and expansion of trade.

5 The EU Budget is financed by contributions from member states and from tariffs (taxes charged) on imports from outside the EU.

6 EU membership may continue to expand as further European countries join.

Benefits of EU membership

Better protection
- The Social Chapter sets out rights and regulations for the workplace.
- Consumer rights are protected throughout the EU; free competition is upheld.

Support
- Aid is directed at poorer regions, including parts of the UK.
- The Common Agricultural Policy helps create security for farmers by buying produce at guaranteed prices. The EU also provides grants to modernise farms.

Easier trade
- People and goods can travel freely across member countries.
- VAT has been harmonised – it cannot fall below 15% in any EU country.
- People can seek jobs throughout the EU.

Environmental standards
- The Common Fisheries Policy controls the amount of fish that countries or individual fishermen can catch.
- Environmental standards (often stricter than British laws) are set for all members.

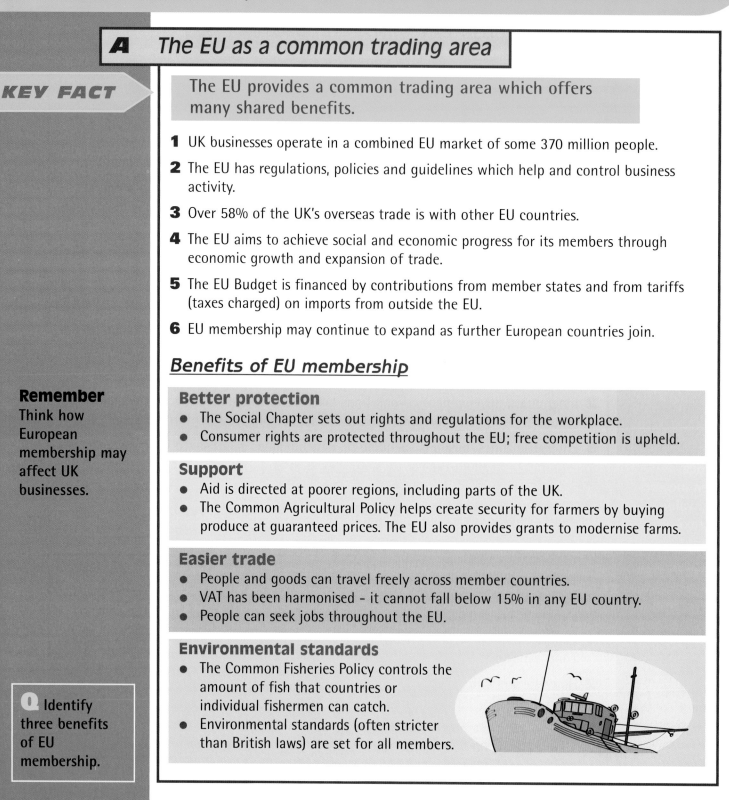

Remember
Think how European membership may affect UK businesses.

Q Identify three benefits of EU membership.

B The Euro as a single currency

The Euro has become a common currency for most EU members but is still being debated in the UK.

In 2002, the Euro became the single currency for most EU member countries. A European central bank supports the system and each country has to keep its economy under strict control. The UK has not yet joined the single currency.

Advantages

- Businesses no longer have to pay a fee to change their money when selling or buying from other countries.

- Businesses no longer need to worry about exchange rate fluctuations when trading across Europe.

- The European Central Bank can make long-term decisions for the benefit of the whole of Europe.

Disadvantages

- Individual countries lose direct control over their economy. A decision which benefits Europe may not be good for an individual country.

- Each country has to abide by tight economic guidelines. This may result in higher unemployment, extra taxes and fewer choices for the government.

Q Name one reason for and one reason against the UK joining the Euro.

PRACTICE

One of the best-known features of the EU is the single market.

1 What is meant by a single market?

2 How does a single market help member countries trade in the EU?

3 Why does the single market persuade foreign firms to set up factories in the EU?

Show that you know there are different views on the Euro and EU membership, using phrases like 'from a large business point of view'.

The global economy

➤ UK businesses compete for world markets.

➤ Changes in the value of the pound affect British firms.

➤ Governments try to boost exports and limit imports.

A UK businesses and world markets

KEY FACT

UK traders face stiff competition in world markets.

Firms selling goods abroad have to compete in worldwide markets, but doing so successfully gives a country the revenue to buy specialist or cheap goods from abroad.

International trade means: ✓

larger markets and lower costs; more opportunities to boost sales; more consumers with diverse tastes.

But it also means: ✗

greater distances for deliveries; customs taxes, paperwork and delays at international borders; the need for different currencies; promotional materials in various languages; different laws and customs to deal with.

Remember
International companies may market the same product in many different countries.

Q What is meant by global competition?

B The importance of exchange rates

KEY FACT

Exchange rate fluctuations will affect British firms who trade abroad.

• The value of the UK pound against other currencies is called its exchange rate.

• UK businesses need foreign currency to trade abroad. Foreign businesses need pounds to buy British goods or invest in British companies.

• As in any other market, increased demand for pounds will push up its 'price'. This affects the price of exports and imports. Frequent changes in the exchange rate create uncertainty for businesses.

• Governments try to keep the exchange rate stable. If there is pressure on the pound because of high demand, the government can supply extra currency from its reserves.

Q Why might a fall in the rate of the £ against the US $ be good for some businesses?

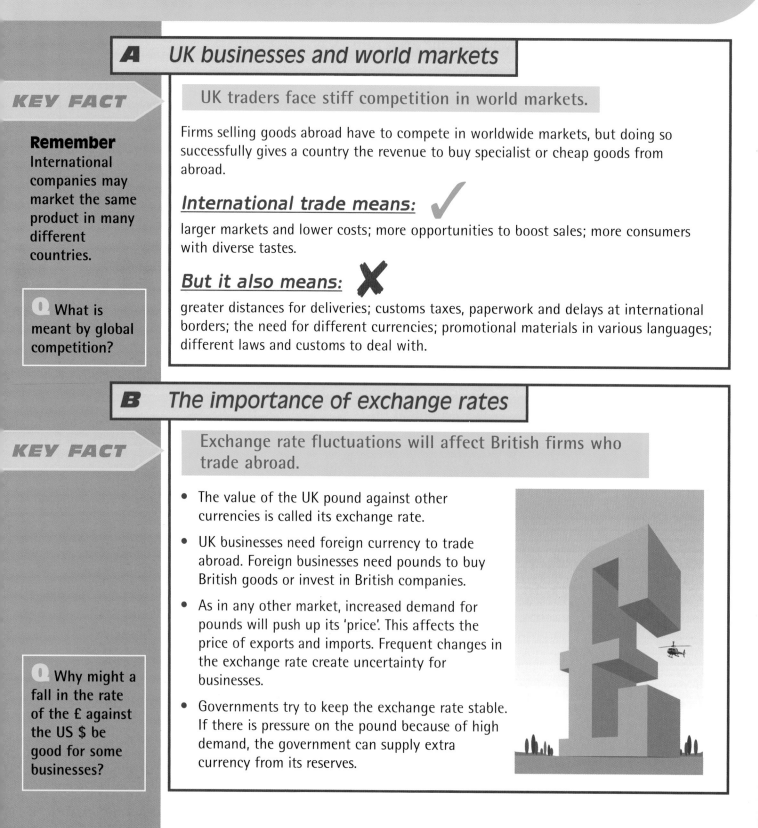

C Government action to promote trade

The government tries to help UK businesses by boosting exports and restricting imports.

- **Imports** are goods and services bought from abroad with payments flowing out to foreign producers.

- UK producers sell **exports** abroad and the money earned comes back into the UK.

- These flows of money are recorded on the country's **balance of payments**.

- The UK usually imports more than it exports. The country has a surplus on trade in services, but a big deficit on trade in goods which means there is an overall **trade deficit**.

Remember
Governments need to work together to encourage trade and stability.

To improve the situation, businesses need to make goods and services more competitive, for instance by investing in training and new technology.

A number of **government measures** can be used to reduce a trade deficit:

- Tariffs (taxes) on imports increase their price and encourage consumers to buy home produce.

- No taxes on exports allows businesses to be competitive in overseas markets.

- Advice to businesses on selling in overseas markets.

- Import quotas restrict imports into the country. Such a policy may lead to retaliatory bans.

Q Name three ways in which the government can help to prevent imports coming into the country.

- Subsidies provide businesses with government money to help keep down their costs and so enable them to charge lower prices than rivals in other countries.

- Exchange control restricts access to foreign currency, making importing and travel more difficult.

- Government advertising campaigns can encourage people to buy home-produced goods and services, while running trade fairs abroad can boost exports.

PRACTICE

Jo runs a craft centre and restaurant near a major tourist attraction in Yorkshire. She expects trade from foreign tourists, especially the Japanese, to increase by 10% in the next six months and by up to 30% in the next year. She is thinking of extending her restaurant.

1 How might Jo's business be affected by:
  a) a decrease in the value of the pound against the yen?
  b) a slump in the Japanese economy?

2 What could the government do to help Jo's business in the long term?

When economic indicators go down, it isn't all bad news. What effects will there be on the costs of imports and exports? Think of the knock-on effects.

Business types & objectives

Provost plc makes animal feed and is in competition with many small businesses operating as sole traders.

a) How might Provost plc differ from sole traders in the following ways:

   i) Ownership?   (2 marks)

   ii) Where to obtain finance to set up the business?   (4 marks)

   iii) Distribution of profits?   (2 marks)

b) State two major business objectives Provost plc might have and explain why they are important to the company.   (4 marks)

(Foundation level)

Model answer

a)

i) Provost will be owned by its many shareholders. These are members of the public who had the cash to buy the shares when they were offered for sale. A sole trader is owned just by the person who set up the business.

ii) Both Provost and a sole trader could finance their business from the owners' funds, but because there may be thousands of shareholders, Provost could raise a larger sum. It could raise further funds by issuing new shares. Provost is a large company and so is likely to borrow larger sums from the bank. The bank can be more certain of getting its money back. Provost may already have assets like a factory, which it could sell and lease back to raise funds.

iii) Shareholders can be paid some of the profits as an annual dividend but Provost's managing board will have to decide if there are enough profits available. These profits may be put back into the business. Different shareholders with different kinds of shares can be given first share of the profits.

The sole trader decides on keeping the profits or putting them into the business.

Why this answer scores full marks

It gives an accurate description of the ownership of both a plc and a sole trader. It makes it clear that, with a plc, it is ownership of shares which gives part ownership of the company. The number of owners is important because it will change the way decisions are made.

The answer concentrates on Provost but makes it clear that it is comparing this with a sole trader. The first section deals with two aspects of finance through shares and is worth two marks. It appears first and is given more importance. The two other points are made simply and clearly.
There is no need to repeat this for the sole trader.

This answer is clear on who decides and who gets the benefit in the two different businesses.

b) **To make profits**: An important business objective as it is usually the overriding reason why people work or invest.

To produce a safe and high quality product: An animal feed business needs to be safe, especially after the BSE scare. A quality product will ensure future buyers.

> The business objectives have been linked to Provost's products. Simple explanations have been used which remind us of some of the different stakeholders.

Other questions

1) The following are features of different kinds of business organisations:

   - Between 2 and 20 owners
   - Issues shares
   - Owners have limited liability
   - Owners usually have unlimited liability

   a) Which two are features of a partnership? (2 marks)

   b) Which two are features of a private limited company? (2 marks)

   c) What is meant by limited liability? (2 marks)

(Foundation level)

2) A sportswear company has a good market share and is competing with foreign firms. The managers believe there is little scope for internal growth and are seeking a merger with another company.

   What are the advantages of growing through a merger rather than by internal growth? (5 marks)

(Higher level)

Business production

Goodwood Ltd makes wooden garden items (sheds, tables and chairs, bird tables and fence panels). These are sold in the factory shop and in garden centres all over England. The company also builds special 'one-off' items at the request of customers.

a) The 'one-off' items are made using 'job production'. State and explain two features of job production. (6 marks)

b) i) Give one reason why job production is NOT suitable for the normal garden items. (2 marks)

   ii) What might be a better method of production for the normal garden items? Why? (6 marks)

c) In November, Goodwood get a new contract from a mail order company for the following:

   - 2000 sheds by August
   - 4000 tables by March
   - 16 000 chairs by March

   Explain how completing the contract would affect production methods and use of labour. (4 marks)

(Foundation level)

Model answer

a) Skilled labour is used because each job requires something different. Each customer wants a different style of chair or table. The job is likely to take longer than making lots of similar items.

b) i) Job production would not be suitable because large amounts of the same item are wanted.
   ii) Batch or mass production would be better because they can use machinery and repeat designs. Workers can train to do a particular job quickly.

c) The contract requires large numbers of similar products. Goodwood needs to switch most workers to batch production. Lots of workers are needed for March but fewer after that, so the business will probably employ workers on a temporary contract.

Why this answer scores full marks

The answers are to the point and linked to the business of garden furniture.

Clear application of the advantages of batch/mass production to the business context.

Good explanation of the consequences of the contract, viewed in two stages: November to March and March to August.

Other questions

1 Kitchen Designs plc makes kitchen units for sale in a range of different designs.

  a) Explain fully how automating the process of production might help the firm. (4 marks)

  b) Interest rates in the UK have fallen to extremely low levels. Explain two ways in which a fall in interest rates might help Kitchen Designs plc. (2 x 5 marks)

(Higher level)

2 An international bridge-building company has, in the past, used expensive models to calculate the size and specification of its bridges using its own highly-trained engineers.

  a) What might be the advantages to this company of using the Internet to find suppliers? (4 marks)

  b) Explain how CAD could help the company in designing a new bridge. (4 marks)

  c) Suggest two problems the company might have in dealing with clients in remote parts of the world and how these problems could be overcome. (4 marks)

(Higher level)

Business finance

Question 1

Study the balance sheet, below, for the company Property Ltd.

a) Fill in the missing figures for working capital and loans. Show your working out.
(4 marks)

b) Give one example of a fixed asset and one of a current liability. (2 marks)

c) Explain the purpose of a balance sheet. (6 marks)

d) Explain the purpose of a profit and loss account. (6 marks)

(Foundation level)

Property Ltd   **Balance sheet** as at 31.3.02

	£000	£000
Fixed assets		140
Current assets		
Stock	40	
Debtors	10	
Cash	50	
	100	
Current liabilities	75	
Working capital	?	
Net assets employed		165
Share capital	50	
Retained profit	60	
Loans (long-term)	?	
Capital employed		165

Model answer

a) Working capital is the amount of capital available to pay immediate debts. This is current assets – current liabilities = £100 000 – £75 000 = £25 000.
Loans + retained profit + share capital = capital employed. Loans + £60 000 + £50 000 = £165 000. Loans = £55 000.

b) Fixed assets are things like equipment. Current liabilities are short-term debts like a bank loan.

c) It shows the financial position of a business at a particular moment. It shows all the liabilities on one side balanced by the assets on the other. It contains important information like the business's ability to pay its debts. This is important to anyone who lends money to the business.

Why this answer scores full marks

The answer shows understanding of key words (1 mark) and identifies correct items from the balance sheet (1 mark). It uses correct units (1 mark) and the calculation is correct (1 mark).

This explanation gives an accurate description, shows some of the key ingredients and explains why they are important.

d) A profit and loss account shows the net profit and is usually published every 6 or 12 months. The total of expenses, losses and overheads are deducted from the sales revenue. A business can check its progress from this account, for example by comparing profits from one year with another, or comparing profits to the volume of sales.

> Again, the key ingredients are mentioned and an example is given of how useful the figures may be in comparing profitability.

Question 2

The finance director at TM Sportswear Ltd has drawn up a cash flow forecast for next year's trading.

Cash flow forecast for TM Sportswear Ltd (£000)				
	Jan-Mar (£000)	Apr-Jun (£000)	Jul-Sep (£000)	Oct-Dec (£000)
Receipts				
Sales	400	500	550	550
Total income	400	500	550	550
Payments				
Suppliers	250	250	275	275
Wages	15	15	15	15
Overheads	120	120	120	120
Total expenditure	385	385	410	410
Net cash flow	15	115	140	140
Opening balance	0	15	130	270
Closing balance	15	130	270	410

Sales at TM Sportswear Ltd for April to June totalled only £360 000 and the directors decide to take out an overdraft to solve this problem.

a) Advise the directors of TM Sportswear Ltd on the amount which should be borrowed and state the reason for your advice. (5 marks)

b) Shortly after taking out an overdraft, the interest rates of all banks increased. Explain how this will be a constraint to TM Sportswear Ltd. (5 marks)

(Foundation level)

Model answer

a) TM Sportswear Ltd should borrow at least £125 000 because there will be a £25 000 shortfall for April–June if all the costings are accurate and there may be a shortfall of £50 000 per period for July–December if the pattern of poorer sales continues. It is possible that sales will pick up nearer Christmas but it is better to be safe than sorry.

Why this answer scores full marks

> The figures are accurate and show an understanding of how a problem may arise during this period and continue in the periods ahead. It makes good use of the case study in the reference to Christmas sales.

b) An increase in interest rates will push up the cost of the loan unless it was agreed at a fixed rate. The bank will expect to receive the interest payment and this may mean a greater cash loss and the business may have to find ways of cutting other costs.

> This shows a clear understanding between interest rate changes and the cost of borrowing. It also provides an example of how the business might take action.

Other questions

1 T-pots Ltd plans to produce 8000 special teapots. It has estimated costs as follows:

Fixed costs: £60 000

Variable costs:	labour	£145 000
	raw materials	£38 000
	power	£15 000
	promotion	£20 000
	other expenses	£10 000
		£228 000

Total costs: **£288 000**

a) Give two examples of fixed costs.   (2 marks)

b) How does a fixed cost differ from a variable cost?   (2 marks)

c) Calculate the total cost of making each teapot. Show your working.   (2 marks)

d) If each teapot sells for £40, how much profit will be made if all 8000 teapots are sold? Show your working.   (4 marks)

(Foundation level)

2 Lena opened an office two years ago and had enough work to employ an assistant. She now has one-year contracts with two large local firms and has had to move to new premises. She has taken on three new employees but has not enough cash to buy computers and office equipment. She is considering leasing the equipment or buying them on Hire Purchase.

a) Describe two features of leasing and two of Hire Purchase.   (4 marks)

b) Which method of obtaining the equipment would you recommend and why?   (6 marks)

(Foundation level)

People in business

Some employees have suggested to their manager that less money should be spent on staff training and on bonuses, and that the saving from this should be used to increase hourly pay rates.

a) Do you think all staff would benefit to the same degree from a general pay rise? (4 marks)

b) Why might this change damage worker motivation? (4 marks)

c) How might the employer gain or lose? (4 marks)

(Foundation level)

Model answer

a) If everyone was working in a similar way on similar jobs, then a general pay rise would be OK. But in many businesses, some workers put in overtime or can work faster for bonuses. They would lose out.

b) Some workers would feel their extra effort is not valued and so not try so hard. Some workers might feel the situation benefits others more than them. Some workers may depend on training for promotion.

c) Basic hourly pay rates are lower than bonuses and overtime. It might cut labour costs and more production might get done in planned working hours. Workers who don't get trained might produce poor work or might leave.

Why this answer scores full marks

The writer shows that there is not a right or wrong answer. It depends on how the business production is organised. The meaning of bonus and hourly pay rate is understood.

The importance of motivation is made clear and it is understood that good effort depends both on the worker and manager. The writer also understands the importance of training to workers.

This shows good understanding of the changes from a business manager's perspective. It makes a connection between cause and effect.

Other questions

1 Jean runs her own clothes design business but needs to appoint an office manager to help run the business.

a) State and explain three duties which the office manager might carry out. (6 marks)

b) State and explain the sequence of events that would lead to the appointment of the office manager. (6 marks)

c) The office manager will be responsible for induction training. How might induction training benefit the business and new employees? (8 marks)

(Higher level)

2 A production manager at a sports goods factory feels the current production line will not cope with an increased range of higher quality products required by customers. He feels this is a good time to update the production process using teamwork and a 'Just-in-time' (JIT) system of stock control.

a) Explain how the introduction of teamwork might affect the performance of the business. (6 marks)

b) Examine the advantages and disadvantages of introducing a JIT system. (9 marks)

(Higher level)

Business and marketing

Question 1

Goodwood Ltd makes wooden garden items (sheds, tables and chairs, bird tables and fence panels). These are sold in the factory shop and in garden centres all over England. The company also builds special 'one-off' items at the request of customers and has recently completed a large order for thousands of garden sheds, tables and chairs from a mail order company. Goodwood Ltd has decided to stop making chairs and tables out of wood but to make them from plastic instead.

Describe the sales promotion and advertising that should be undertaken in the short term. (8 marks)

(Higher level)

Model answer

Goodwood Ltd may lose customers who prefer traditional wooden furniture. The company should promote the new plastic items at the point of sale in garden centres and send brochures to other mail order companies to win new orders. They might even choose to run an advert in a national newspaper with links to the various garden centres.

The advert could show a typical family enjoying the furniture in the garden and appeal to fun-loving families as well as those who like tasteful garden furniture.

Why this answer scores full marks

It gives a reason why promotion is necessary (2 marks).

It gives several different suggestions (2 marks each) for the campaign and refers to a typical target audience.

Question 2

Many supermarkets stock their shelves with own brand products which sit alongside other well-known brands of goods.

a) Using two examples, explain what is meant by the term 'brand'. (4 marks)

b) Why do you think supermarkets sell their own brand label products as well as branded goods? (4 marks)

c) Outline and explain a strategy that a national supermarket chain might use to compete with its main rivals.

(6 marks)

(Foundation level)

Model answer

a) A brand is the name given to a product to make it appear different to rivals. Timotei shampoo and Kellogg's Corn Flakes are examples.

b) Own brands can help a supermarket capture market share and improve the firm's image. They also allow supermarkets to compete with each other and may help to increase company profits.

c) A supermarket might run a loss-leading campaign with low prices on a few key products to win customers. They might then sell extra numbers of other goods. The supermarket could also offer loyalty cards with bonuses if the customers keep coming back to the store. A store might also offer to deliver goods locally which have been ordered over the Internet.

Why this answer scores full marks

Accurate explanation with relevant examples.

Four points are included in this tightly packed answer. An example might have been included.

This answer has three different examples which fit into a sensible strategy to win customers from other supermarkets. Each suggestion has an example of how it might affect customers.

Other questions

1 Elegant Kitchens plc intends to try to increase the sales of its 'Farmhouse' range of kitchen units by marketing it to middle and lower income groups.

   a) Name four elements of the marketing mix.   (4 marks)

   b) Suggest a marketing strategy which might be used by Elegant Kitchens plc to increase sales of the 'Farmhouse' range to the middle and lower income groups.   (8 marks)

(Higher level)

2 A business manager decides to use market research before trying to expand the business.

   a) What is market research?   (3 marks)

   b) How might the market research be carried out?   (3 marks)

   c) Why does market research sometimes fail?   (4 marks)

(Higher level)

The business environment

Many products are advertised as being 'environmentally friendly'. Some of these same products are sold in elaborate packaging. Claims made by businesses for their products have not always been checked out.

a) Explain two ways in which a product could be 'environmentally friendly'. (4 marks)

b) Why do firms often use large amounts of resources in packaging products? (4 marks)

c) What are the costs to society of using resources for packaging? (4 marks)

d) Why might the government and the European Union pass laws to protect the consumer? (6 marks)

(Foundation level)

Model answer

a) Two points could be chosen from: recyclable, not tested on animals, efficient production, no dangerous materials.

b) Firms use lots of resources on packaging because it can improve the quality of the product, especially if freshness is important. The packaging can make the product stand out from other similar products. It may also be necessary to package some products safely, such as a kitchen knife.

c) Lots of plastic packaging can add to problems of waste disposal and pollution. The materials may also be made from non-renewable resources and of course the resources could be used for something else. There is an opportunity cost.

d) The government could pass laws to make companies protect the environment and to provide better information on the labels explaining how care is being taken in the production of the product. Some businesses may spend more money than others and find it harder to compete. Therefore laws can provide a 'level playing field' for everyone.

Why this answer scores full marks

Each relevant point needs to be linked to the idea of 'environmentally friendly'.

This answer provides a good explanation of why packaging may be used, and makes use of examples.

Simple examples are given and the use of specialist terms strengthens the answer.

Examples of government laws are mentioned with reasons as to how they might help.

Other question

1) Explain the advantages and disadvantages to a large UK transport company of membership of the European Union. (10 marks)

(Higher level)

Topic checker

- After you've revised a topic, go through these questions.
- Put a tick if you know the answer, a cross if you don't (you can check your answer at the bottom of each section).
- Try the questions again until you've got a column that are all ticks! Then you'll know you can be confident.

Business types & objectives

1 What is meant by a 'secondary sector' business?	☐ ☐ ☐
2 What is meant by 'horizontal integration'?	☐ ☐ ☐
3 What is a 'sole trader'?	☐ ☐ ☐
4 How many partners can there be in a partnership?	☐ ☐ ☐
5 What is a 'deed of partnership'?	☐ ☐ ☐
6 What does 'limited liability' mean?	☐ ☐ ☐
7 What is the major difference between a 'Ltd' and a 'plc'?	☐ ☐ ☐
8 What is a 'co-operative'?	☐ ☐ ☐
9 Why is a franchise often a good way of starting up in business?	☐ ☐ ☐
10 What are the main reasons for privatising a public sector organisation?	☐ ☐ ☐
11 What is meant by 'chain of command' in a business organisation?	☐ ☐ ☐
12 What is meant by 'span of control' in a business organisation?	☐ ☐ ☐
13 What is the name of the department which looks after the people in a business?	☐ ☐ ☐
14 Identify a business objective apart from making a profit.	☐ ☐ ☐
15 Who are the 'stakeholders' in a business?	☐ ☐ ☐

Answers 1 Businesses using raw materials to produce finished goods 2 When a business links to another in the same sector 3 A business owned and controlled by one person 4 Between 2 and 20 5 A set of rules to ensure good behaviour between partners 6 Owners are liable only for the money they have invested in the business 7 Shares in a Ltd are only available to original founders and their friends, not to the general public 8 A business run for the benefit of the stakeholders with each person having an equal share in it 9 The risks are minimised because the franchiser supports the franchisee as the business sets up 10 To bring more competition and private finance into the business 11 The line of command from top to bottom in a business 12 The amount of responsibility of any particular person in a business 13 Human Resource department 14 To provide a service; to be charitable 15 People who have an interest in the business: includes managers, owners, customers, workers, local and national communities

Business production

16 What is meant by 'customer-led' production?	☐	☐	☐
17 Why is a wide product range important?	☐	☐	☐
18 What are 'economies of scale'?	☐	☐	☐
19 What is the difference between batch and flow production methods?	☐	☐	☐
20 How can teamwork improve job satisfaction?	☐	☐	☐
21 What is the major benefit of 'just-in-time' production?	☐	☐	☐
22 What is meant by an increase in 'productivity'?	☐	☐	☐
23 What is meant by 'automation'?	☐	☐	☐
24 What is 'CAD'?	☐	☐	☐
25 Why is research and development important for quality control?	☐	☐	☐
26 What is 'total quality management' (TQM)?	☐	☐	☐
27 Why might a sawmill be likely to locate near a forest?	☐	☐	☐
28 Why is a small shop likely to locate away from a big shopping mall?	☐	☐	☐
29 How can a government encourage a business to move to a Greenfield site?	☐	☐	☐
30 Why might a government stop a business moving to a particular site?	☐	☐	☐

Answers 16 Production where customer preferences determine what is made 17 It spreads the risk of failure when a product doesn't sell 18 Cost savings which come from making the product on a large scale 19 Batch production uses large scale to make a batch of one item before switching to another item; flow is a continuous production of identical items 20 Workers are more involved with production decisions as they work together 21 It cuts the costs of storing unnecessary stock levels 22 An increase in the amount produced by each worker 23 Production is done completely by machine 24 Computer-aided design, typically used where design models are important 25 R&D can generate new ideas or new ways of producing goods to high quality 26 Everyone is involved in quality management from the beginning to the end of the process 27 Because the wood is nearby, it can be cut down to size immediately, making it easier to transport to market 28 Because rates and other costs are very high in big shopping centres 29 By offering grants to businesses which move 30 Because the business might spoil an area of beauty or bring pollution

Business finance

31 Why is financial planning important to a business?	☐ ☐ ☐
32 What is meant by an 'internal source' of finance?	☐ ☐ ☐
33 Why is a bank loan usually preferred to a bank overdraft?	☐ ☐ ☐
34 What is 'trade credit'?	☐ ☐ ☐
35 What are 'running costs'?	☐ ☐ ☐
36 What are 'expansion costs'?	☐ ☐ ☐
37 What is a 'business plan'?	☐ ☐ ☐
38 What is meant by a 'break-even' point for a business?	☐ ☐ ☐
39 What is the difference between fixed and variable costs?	☐ ☐ ☐
40 What is meant by 'margin of safety' when talking about production levels?	☐ ☐ ☐
41 What is a 'cash flow forecast'?	☐ ☐ ☐
42 Why is a profit and loss account important?	☐ ☐ ☐
43 What does a balance sheet show?	☐ ☐ ☐
44 What is meant by the 'working capital' of a business?	☐ ☐ ☐
45 Why is an acid test ratio important?	☐ ☐ ☐

Answers 31 It helps to keep costs under control and to allow for unexpected events 32 Finance found from within the business, usually from retained profits 33 Because rates of interest are usually lower on loans 34 Where goods bought are paid for at a later date 35 The regular costs of producing goods or services, e.g. wages 36 The costs of expanding a business, such as buying a new factory or machinery 37 A plan of the predicted performance of a business, usually prepared for a lender 38 The point at which the costs of production are just met by sales revenue 39 Variable costs change with the amount of customers or sales; fixed costs don't 40 The amount of spare money available because revenue is greater than costs 41 A prediction of the cash flowing in and out of the business over the next year 42 Provides managers and others with a record of all the revenue and costs during the last accounting period (usually a year) 43 A snapshot showing all the assets and liabilities of a business 44 The finance immediately available for running the business (current assets – current liabilities) 45 It shows how easily a business could cover its short-term debts

People in business

46 Why is 'Maslow's hierarchy' important to personnel managers?	☐ ☐ ☐
47 Apart from money, what is a major reason for going to work?	☐ ☐ ☐
48 What is meant by a non-financial incentive to work hard?	☐ ☐ ☐
49 What is meant by 'performance-related pay'?	☐ ☐ ☐
50 Why are job descriptions important to employers and employees?	☐ ☐ ☐
51 What is 'induction training'?	☐ ☐ ☐
52 What is 'off-the-job training'?	☐ ☐ ☐
53 Why are government training schemes important?	☐ ☐ ☐
54 Why are good external communications important to a business?	☐ ☐ ☐
55 Why are written communications important within a business?	☐ ☐ ☐
56 Why is e-mail important in a large company?	☐ ☐ ☐
57 What is meant by 'industrial relations'?	☐ ☐ ☐
58 What are Trade Unions?	☐ ☐ ☐
59 Why are health and safety laws important to business?	☐ ☐ ☐
60 What is 'collective bargaining'?	☐ ☐ ☐

Answers 46 It provides a guide for motivating people: take care of basic needs first and then think about job satisfaction and higher needs 47 Because many people see work as a source of personal satisfaction and self-esteem 48 Things like praise and the opportunity for promotion which makes a person try harder 49 Pay is linked to the achievement of agreed targets 50 Because they clarify exactly what is expected of a person in any job 51 Training to help new employees settle into a workplace 52 Training which takes place away from the workplace 53 Because they provide support for employees to help them move jobs or to retrain with new skills Businesses cannot always afford to pay for such training 54 These are the links between a business and its customers or its suppliers; customers will not buy the products of a business which treats them badly 55 They provide a permanent record of communications; especially important when the issues are the subject of disagreement 56 It helps to speed up communication between employees and saves time and money 57 The relationship between the workforce and the management of a business 58 Organisations that look after the interests of workers in a particular 'trade' or kind of business 59 They make sure every business has proper health and safety procedures in place; they set standards for every business 60 A process of negotiation which involves every side with an interest in the result

Business and marketing

61 What is the importance of a SWOT analysis to a business?	☐ ☐ ☐
62 What is meant by a 'market segment'?	☐ ☐ ☐
63 What is the difference between primary and secondary data used in market research?	☐ ☐ ☐
64 What is a survey based on quotas?	☐ ☐ ☐
65 What are the 'four Ps' of the marketing mix?	☐ ☐ ☐
66 Why will the marketing mix vary from business to business?	☐ ☐ ☐
67 What is the major advantage and disadvantage of advertising via national TV networks?	☐ ☐ ☐
68 What is meant by a 'product life cycle'?	☐ ☐ ☐
69 Why is the product life cycle for a computer game different to that of a product like salt?	☐ ☐ ☐
70 Name one way in which the life cycle of a product can be extended.	☐ ☐ ☐
71 What is the major advantage of branding to a company?	☐ ☐ ☐
72 What is likely to happen to the price of a product if demand is greater than supply?	☐ ☐ ☐
73 What is meant by 'skimming' as a pricing policy?	☐ ☐ ☐
74 What is meant by 'direct mailing' as part of the promotion of a product?	☐ ☐ ☐
75 Why is packaging seen by some businesses as adding value to a product?	☐ ☐ ☐

Answers 61 It provides a breakdown of the strengths and weaknesses of the business and of opportunities to expand in the future 62 A division of a business's potential market based on their different characteristics, e.g sex, age, location, income and lifestyle 63 Primary data is collected at first hand, secondary data is collected and published by someone else 64 Where data is collected from a pre-determined set of people; the interviewer has to ask a given number of people from each market segment 65 Price, promotion, product, place 66 Because each business will have different needs, e.g. some may wish to compete mainly by price rather than through advertising 67 Reaches a national audience but can be expensive 68 The different stages of a product from initial development through to closure after loss of sales 69 A computer game sells for a limited period while it is in fashion; salt is always wanted for cooking and there is no obvious replacement for it 70 By extra advertising; by widening the product range; by changing the product image 71 It distinguishes your product from that of rivals 72 The price will rise because consumers are keen to get hold of the product 73 Charging high prices while a product is new and fashionable; the price is often then dropped to attract other consumers 74 Direct mailing means sending promotional leaflets directly to the homes of consumers or to business customers 75 Packaging can 'add value' if the final product is seen to be worth more to the consumer

The business environment

**7t.

79 What is the role of the Competition Commission?

80 What is an external cost of business?

81 Give two examples of the external benefits of a business locating in an area.

82 Give two examples of government policy which affect businesses.

83 What is 'income tax'?

84 What is 'value added tax' and who pays it?

85 What is the 'European Union'?

86 Identify three benefits of EU membership.

87 What is the 'Euro'?

88 What is meant by 'global trade'?

89 What is the meaning of 'the £ has gone up against the $'?

90 What are 'tariffs'?

Answers **76** Business rivals; government; pressure groups
77 Helps to keep down costs; encourages new products
78 Passes laws like the Trade Descriptions Act; provides agencies like the Trading Standards Office
79 Investigates businesses which have a large share of any market to make sure they are behaving well **80** A cost to the community which is not paid for by the business **81** Business employees bring extra spending into the community; the business may develop a local road to everyone's benefit
82 Policies which help to bring lower interest rates and so make borrowing cheaper; the government takes tax from businesses which can be used to help poorer people in the community **83** A tax taken from every worker's pay, linked to how much they earn; very low wages are not taxed at all
84 A tax on spending which covers most goods and services; everyone who buys the goods pays the tax **85** The EU is a common trading area for member countries **86** Easier trade between members as there are no taxes when crossing borders; a shared currency; consumer protection laws which apply across the EU **87** The common European currency which has replaced national currencies for most EU members
88 Taking part in trade across continents **89** The exchange rate of the £ has gone up compared with that of the $; a customer with £s can now buy more US goods for the same money **90** A tax on imports used by governments to protect their own businesses from foreign imports

Complete the facts

Business types & objectives

1 Complete the following table.

Business sector	Kind of business activity
Primary	
	Using raw materials to produce finished goods
Tertiary	

2 Complete the following chain of production with appropriate examples.

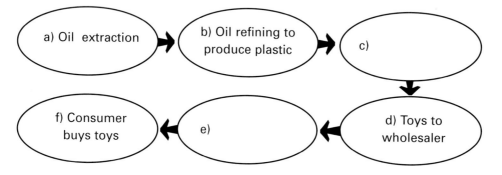

3 Complete the table below.

	Sole trader	Partnership
Decision making	Sole responsibility	
Profits		Shared between partners
Start-up finance	Needs to find all the finance	
Liability	Unlimited	

4 Complete the diagram showing features of companies.

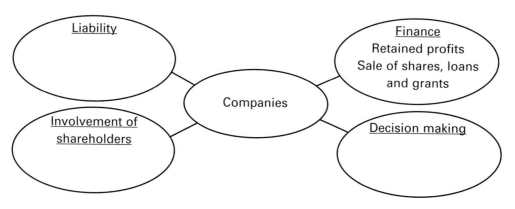

5 Complete the following table.

Advantages of developing a hotel chain through franchising:

	Benefits for hotel company (franchiser)	Benefits for local manager (franchisee)
Start-up	Business grows without large debts.	Less risk during start-up.
Profits		Keeps most of profits (% might go to franchiser).
Management	Only central management needed. Less hassle than opening new branch.	
Training and quality	Provide central training, but get people with local knowledge. Ensure quality standards.	

6 Complete the following business organisation chart.

Purchasing Manager, Production-design Manager, Managing Director, Quality Control Manager, Production Planning Manager, Production Director, Marketing Director

7 Match the following stakeholders with their objectives.

	Repeat orders and reliable payment
	Local jobs and clean environment
	Good pay, job satisfaction and security
	Good return on investment
	Value for money
	Good salary, status and successful department

Customers   Employees   Managers   Suppliers   Shareholders   Local community

Business production

8 Complete the table below.

Product choice	Examples	Advantages	Disadvantages
Business with sole product	Toy firm just making balls	Good if product in great demand	
Business with wide product range			Difficult to manage Can raise costs
Business with wide product mix	Unilever: makes food and cleaning products, etc.		

9 Match the following types of economies of scale with their meanings.

Managerial   Trading   Financial   Technical

	Using machinery more efficiently (five small firms, five fork lift drivers: one large firm, three fork lift drivers)
	Buying materials in bulk so unit cost falls
	Borrowing larger sums of money at lower rates of interest
	Large firm able to hire specialist managers

10 Complete the following table showing methods of production.

	Advantages	Disadvantages
Job production Example:	High quality product made by skilled workers Job satisfaction high Easy to isolate problem areas	
		Costly storage needed Some repetition in jobs Batches need to be moved Machinery needs resetting
Flow production Example:	Large output, low unit cost	Large investment in machinery Inflexible assembly line Repetitive work, poor motivation Products all the same Breakdowns cause big problems

Engine assembly   Bodywork shaping   Wheel and seats   Body fitted to chassis   Final parts added
                   and spraying   on chassis

11 Show where in the production line the following parts would need to be delivered under a Just-in-time (JIT) scheme:

a) tyres   b) metal for car body   c) seat covers   d) paint for body

e) engine blocks f) windscreen   g) headlights   h) wheel suspension

12 Complete the bubbles to show what each of these three groups expects of a high quality product. One example for each has been done for you.

Business managers

* A product which is better than other firms' products

*

*

Customers

* A product which lasts a long time

*

*

Government

* A product which passes safety checks

*

*

13 Why might each of the following be important to a business when choosing a location?

a) Labour

b) Raw materials and the market

c) Climate

d) Cost of land

e) Roads

f) Government grants

Business finance

14 Complete this table comparing internal and external sources of finance and their main uses. (The missing source answers are given below.)

Grants, Retained profits, Bank overdrafts, Investments, Lease of assets, Trade credit, Hire purchase

Source	Features	Used for
Internal		
	Money earned. No interest to pay, easily available. Most common source of finance.	Running costs first. Also, potentially, renewal and expansion.
	Money put in by owners or, if a limited company, obtained by selling shares. Usually long-term commitment.	
	A 'one-off' for raising money, generally when a business is struggling.	
External		
	Money can be withdrawn, even if little in the bank already. Short-term agreements, high interest charged.	Covering gaps in cash flow.
Loans	Money from banks or other sources. Arranged to cover different time periods, with different interest rates. Often need guarantees to ensure pay-back.	
	Money from government, generally tied in to fixed commitments such as improving a region's unemployment or environment.	
	Buying goods, but not paying for them until an agreed later date.	
	Payments are spread over time, so less money committed in the short term. Interest is charged, but item (e.g. equipment) eventually owned outright.	Buying equipment, renewal.

15 Complete the contents page for a business plan which is being sent by two partners hoping for a bank loan to start up a florists.

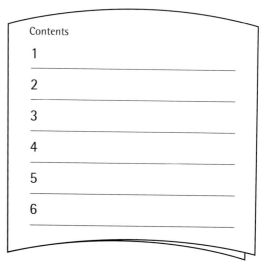

Contents

1 _____

2 _____

3 _____

4 _____

5 _____

6 _____

16 Study the graph below and then complete the sentences that follow.

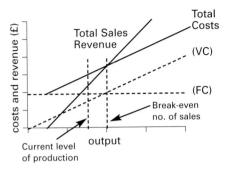

a) The break-even point shows

_____

b) The business will make a profit when

_____

c) Profit is shown in the graph by the area

_____

d) At the current production level the business will make a loss because

_____

e) The business could become more profitable if it

_____

17a) Complete the following cash flow forecast. All figures are in £s.

	January	February	March	April
Cash in	10 000	10 000	4000	3000
minus				
Cash out	8500	6500	5000	5000
=				
Net cash flow	1500	3500	-1000	*
plus				
Opening balance	2500	4000	*	*
=				
Closing balance	4000	*	*	*

17b) What does this chart tell you about the cash flow for January to April?

_____

17c) If this business is to be successful in the months ahead, what must happen to the net cash during May to December?

_____

18 Complete the following profit and loss account. Write notes in the boxes to explain what the figures show.

Profit and loss account for year ended 31 Mar 2002

	£000
Sales revenue	20 500
(-) Cost of sales	14 200
Gross profit	
(+) Other income	500
(-) Overheads	4500
Net profit	
(-) Tax	1000
Profits after tax	3100
Dividends paid	1800
Retained profit	

19 Complete the following balance sheet. Write notes in the boxes to explain what the figures show.

Balance sheet as at 31 Mar 2002

	£000	£000
Assets		
Fixed assets		3400
Current assets		
Stock	800	
Debtors	2100	
Cash	2000	
	*	
Liabilities		
Current liabilities	3800	
Net current assets (working capital)		*
Net assets employed		*
Long-term liabilities	1800	
		2700
Capital & reserves		
Share capital		1700
Retained profit		*
Capital employed		2700

20 Complete the table below explaining the importance of each ratio. Who would be interested in such information and why?

Ratio	What does it show?	Who might be interested?
Gross profit margin 15%	That the gross profit is 15p for every £1 of sales.	Managers because they want to see how the firm is performing. Creditors because they want to see good profits to get loans repaid.
Current ratio 3:1		
Acid test ratio 1:1		

People in business

21 As a Human Resource Manager, you have been asked to recommend a new pay and benefit scheme for your sales staff. Identify three ways in which you will pay your staff and three other kinds of benefit which you will offer. Add one sentence on each to explain why these will be good for staff.

Idea	This will be good because ...
Pay 1) Pay 2) Pay 3)	
Benefit 1) Benefit 2) Benefit 3)	

22 Order the following job recruitment procedures in the boxes below.

a) Check references.

b) Compare applications to the person specification to arrive at a shortlist for interview.

c) Monitor the performance of the new staff member through an appraisal system.

d) Draw up the job description and the person specification.

e) Interview the candidates; select the most suitable person.

f) Advertise the job.

g) Draw up a contract and arrange induction training.

Step 1 → Step 2 → Step 3 → Step 4 → Step 5 → Step 6 → Step 7

23 Complete the following table to show the main advantages and disadvantages of training for both employers and employees.

	Advantages	Disadvantages
Employer	• • •	• Training costs money and time • •
Employee	• Provides extra job satisfaction • •	• • •

24 Explain why the following communication channels are appropriate for each task.

Channel of communication	Task	Reason
Memo	A manager's reminder to her secretary to arrange a meeting	
E-mail	A short instruction about a new product to be sent to 120 sales staff	
Telephone call	A follow-up to a customer complaint about a product	
Meeting with all staff	Latest information about staff redundancies	

25 Use the words below to complete the following sentences about industrial relations.

decent pay   workers   lateness   profit   employers   costs

job security   job roles   relations   issues   responsibility   pay

- A successful business needs .... and .... who respect each others' rights and a decision-making process which ensures fair play.

- Industrial .... is the term used to describe the relationship between the workforce and the management of a business. Good relationships mean that difficult .... can be sorted out openly and fairly.

- In any business, issues involving staff and management might be small day-to-day ones like .... or sorting out .... Other important issues like .... or the introduction of new working methods, affect the whole workforce.

- Businesses, especially large ones, need good organisation and a clear line of .... so that everyone knows what to do or who to talk to if problems arise.

- Everyone wants their business to be a success, but employers may be more concerned about cutting .... and selling products for .... Workers may be more concerned about decent .... and .... Both groups have to balance the protection of their own interests with their shared concern to produce goods on time for customers.

Business and marketing

26 List the advantages and disadvantages of using the following types of data for research.

Primary data (original)	Secondary data (published)
•	• Wide range of data available
•	•
• Can target specific market segments	•
•	•
•	•

27 Match the following items to their correct section in the marketing mix.

* Improve the quality of the product.
* Increase expenditure on advertising.
* Use posters, adverts and local leafleting.
* Develop new range of products.
* Improve after-sales service.
* Offer discounts.
* Have different prices for different customers.

* Update the product features.
* Use a loss-leader to attract customers.
* Change the timing of adverts.
* Advertise in the press; on TV; at point-of-sale.
* Change the size and packaging.
* Adjust basic price level.
* Choose to sell through supermarkets.
* Change delivery times and stock levels.

Product	Place
Promotion	**Price**

28a) Place the following labels in the correct place on the product life cycle diagram.

Saturation   Launch   Decline   Maturity   Growth

Hi-tech products such as computers tend to have a short life cycle, as new developments quickly make old machines outdated. Standard essentials, such as salt and soap, generally have very long cycles.

Rapid growth is likely as the product gets established in the market.

A mature product is well set, but other similar products are now coming onto the scene. Without the same development costs, competitions are likely to be charging a lower price.

A saturated market has so many products that there is no longer room for growth.

When new products begin to appear, the original market goes into decline.

SALES

TIME

28b) List five ways in which the life of a product could be extended.

i)

ii)

iii)

iv)

v)

29 Match the following pricing policies with their definitions.

Loss-leader   Cost-plus pricing   Consumer-led pricing

Price discrimination   Competitive pricing   Skimming (or creaming) the market

Policy	Definition
	Add a mark-up to the total cost of each product
	Set price close to those of competitors
	Set price at or below cost (with no mark-up) in order to penetrate a new market
	Set a high price while the product is fashionable
	Charge different prices to different people for the same product
	Set prices which consumers are happy to pay as reasonable value for money

The business environment

30 Give one example of each of the following external forces working on a business.

External influence	Example
Business rivals taking advantage of new technology to bring out a new product	
An industry setting guidelines for all the businesses in that sector	

Customers' tastes changing	
Government introduces a new law affecting business	
Pressure group campaigns against business because of environmental damage	
A slump in another country affects UK business	

31 Match the following agencies to their work in protecting consumers.

Trading Standards Officers   Office of Fair Trading   UK Government   ABTA

British Standards Institute   Citizens' Advice Bureaux   Environmental Health Officers

	Check on faulty products, and weights and measures.
	Tests products for safety and quality. Issues 'Kitemarks' to show that a product has met certain standards.
	Provides information and advice leaflets.
	Check on such things as food hygiene, pollution and illegal waste disposal.
	Promises to get customers home from holiday if a firm goes bust.
	Passes laws protecting the consumer.
	Provide free advice and help people to make complaints.

32 Read the following passage about the government's management of the economy. Fill in the spaces with the words below.

taxes   risky   benefits   growth   confidence   prices

cycle   sales   demand   planning   consumers

- The activities of a business may be affected by government policies and by the state of the national economy in general. Businesses expect governments to steer the economy towards steady .... and to avoid big changes in ...., interest rates and exchange rates.

- In the UK, we expect our government to make sure businesses operate fairly but also to provide some goods and services for .... We expect the government to ensure the poorest are helped by the better-off through .... and ....

- The government tries to smooth out the big ups and downs in the business ....

- Growth in UK business output averages 2-3% a year but it tends to fluctuate in cycles every four to five years. Growth and employment are helped by high .... in the economy. If demand outstrips supply, there can be a general increase in prices (inflation) and business .... becomes very difficult. If the government raises taxes, it can reduce demand but at the risk of pushing up unemployment and shaking the .... of businesses.

- Rising prices affect jobs with fewer goods bought by consumers leading to falling .... and cut backs on employment. Workers may want more pay to cover higher prices and so there is extra upward pressure on business costs.

- The government can help but it can't control all the factors which make business a .... activity.

Business types & objectives (page 85)

1. a) Between 2 and 20 owners; Owners usually have unlimited liability.
   b) Issues shares; Owners have limited liability.
   c) Owners risk losing only the value of the shares they bought, not all of their other assets.
2. A merger can take place quickly and can bring together the strengths of two businesses. It can give this company very quick access to other markets through the merged company and does not have to cost a lot of money. It can also spread the risk of business between the two companies.

Business production (page 86)

1. a) Machinery could be used to make standard kitchen units to a high standard. The machinery would initially cost a lot but could then work 24 hours a day and be very productive. Machinery would probably be quicker than humans. Orders could also be made to suit customers. Computer controls will help to spot breakdowns and should be very efficient.
   b) If Kitchen Designs plc has taken out a loan, it means it could afford to borrow more as the cost of repayments will be lower. This would mean that the company could afford to invest more in machinery and expand the company with confidence. A fall in interest rates may also encourage consumers to borrow and spend more knowing that their credit card repayments might also fall a little. They might pay for larger items like a new house or a new kitchen rather than put it off for better times. This would mean more business for the company.
2. a) It could find a supplier who provides materials at a lower cost, or who has a good reputation. It could search worldwide for such a supplier and, with more competition, the business should get a good deal.
   b) The computer allows the engineers to build virtual models and try them out with sophisticated tests. This saves the time and money involved in building actual models, although training the engineers to use the software will require an initial investment. The company should be able to adjust the programme to any design.
   c) The company representatives wouldn't meet the clients face to face and might not understand all of their needs without site visits. This may mean it is difficult to form a close and trusting

relationship. There may need to be a lot of information exchanged. E-mail and video-conferencing would help this process as well as visits.

Business finance (page 89)

1. a) Fixed costs can be the cost of hiring or buying a factory, and the equipment which goes into it.
   b) Variable costs change as more goods are produced; fixed costs stay the same even if there is no production at all.
   c) TC = FC + VC = £60 000 + £145 000 + £38 000 + £15 000 + £20 000 + £10 000 = £288 000.
   d) TR = £8000 @ £40 = £320 000;
   Profit = TR-TC = £320 000 - £288 000 = £32 000.
2. a) Leasing means 'borrowing' the computers in return for a fee. The computers would be maintained by the business who leases them to Lena. If Lena uses hire purchase, she is buying the computers over a period of time. A finance company will lend the money and Lena will take ownership when she has paid back a certain percentage. She will pay more than a straight purchase but the computers will be available immediately.
   b) Leasing may be the better option because she is not certain to keep the contracts for the business in a year's time and may have to 'downsize' again. If she does need to expand, or to update the computers, she can renegotiate the terms of the lease.

People in business (page 90)

1. a) Oversee all the paperwork, which might include liaising with customers outside of the business; manage the office and link with other managers in the business; take responsibility for the finances, including the day to day documentation and drawing up accounts at the end of the year.
   b) There would need to be a job and a person specification drawn up with the help of other key staff. The job would have to be advertised in appropriate places, like fashion magazines, and a shortlist for interview drawn up. Candidates may be given a test to show they can manage an office and business links. The most suitable candidate would be offered the job, once references had been checked. Some training and an introductory period would be set to make sure everyone is happy.
   c) Induction training makes sure all new staff understand their roles and what is expected of

them. This avoids silly mistakes which could lose customers and also helps the new person to fit in. The training may motivate the new person and encourage them to stay. They pick up new skills and the company gets a good worker and a reputation as a good employer. In-house training is probably better than off-the-job training for this task.

2 a) Once a team is established, it is likely to encourage better work and increase motivation among staff. A team can support each other and may solve small problems without any breaks in production. The team may become multi-skilled and work on a more flexible basis. On the other hand, it will take time to establish and may not suit all workers. There will also be training costs.

   b) A JIT system will mean that raw materials and parts arrive just in time for assembly purposes and the factory will not be cluttered with unnecessary piles of material. This should cut costs provided everything comes in on time. On the downside, it will require very reliable suppliers who know the business well and can deliver to time. If not, the sports factory will be at a standstill and customers will experience delays. Computers can help with communication and stock records ensuring that the system is not hard to support.

Business and marketing (page 92)

1 a) Price, promotion, product and place.
   b) They could use a competitive pricing strategy, or perhaps even a cut price strategy, to gain the attention of their target market. They could also research what kind of kitchen units this particular group likes and target production to meet these needs. Advertisements in the magazines read by such customers, offering a special price for those who place an order by a certain date, could also help. This would give the business a good start. It may wish to sell through DIY outlets which could give the units a good display and suggest high quality.

2 a) Market research describes the methods used by a business to find out what customers' needs are and what products they prefer. It may also provide an insight into competitor activity.
   b) Research could be desk-based using published secondary data. This approach is good when there are lots of trade publications and statistics collected on the particular product and market. Otherwise, surveys may have to be carried out by direct questionnaires, post or telephone. Researchers will be paid to collect and process this primary data.
   c) Market research sometimes fails because the wrong questions are asked or because the

information collected is incomplete or done in a hurry. There may not be a big enough source of finance to pay for the expensive collection of new data. If the product is very new, there are likely to be risks because no-one is sure they want the product. The recent failure of ITV Digital is a good example.

The business environment (page 93)

1 The EU can offer many advantages to a transport firm because they have to cross a lot of international boundaries to carry out their business. There would be no delays while frontier checks were made across the EU borders. The common currency and simplified paperwork with common rules should make most business deals easier to manage. Fuel prices and taxes should be roughly the same and so competition between European firms is fair. The EU would make sure that no other company behaved unfairly.

But the company would have to make sure they meet all the rules themselves and there are a lot of checks regarding transport vehicles. There are also rules about distances to travel and, of course, while EU doors are open to a UK firm, so too UK doors are now open to all sorts of competing firms. The EU has rules about employment and it may mean the UK firm has to change the way some drivers are employed. The UK has not yet joined the common currency, the Euro, so other European drivers may have an advantage with few currency problems. At the moment, taxes on fuel and roads are different between countries, so it may be difficult to compete in the short term.

Business types & objectives

Pages 8/9

Q A chain of production shows how different business types can be linked together.

Q The tertiary sector is the most important by size and by employment, but other sectors are vital in providing raw materials and finished products.

Q Wood from trees (primary), manufacture of shed (secondary), shed sold in garden centre (tertiary).

Q Distribution.

Practice questions

1 a) Secondary b) Primary c) Tertiary d) Tertiary.
2 a) Vertical b) Horizontal.

Pages 10/11

Q Sole trader: a business owned and controlled by one person; Partnership: a business owned and controlled by between 2 and 20 partners.

Q Permission to trade; VAT registration; produce key financial accounts; follow health and safety rules.

Q Unlimited liability; lack of capital; pressure of responsibility.

Practice questions

1 a) John could lose all his assets, including his house, if the business went bust.
   b) John and his friend are joint owners of the business and are both liable for any debts.
2 a) You make all the decisions, keep all the profits and have the satisfaction of doing things your own way.
   b) The owners haven't planned the finances carefully enough; the business isn't successfully managed; the marketing is poor, or the products are not popular.

Pages 12/13

Q Limited liability means that if a business goes bust, the owners only lose the money they contributed to the business and no more.

Q Plcs are usually larger, well-known businesses. Banks believe they are more likely to repay debts and so are more willing to lend to them.

Q AGMs and annual reports are important because they are part of the process which makes the company accountable to the owners. Everyone can see that the business practices are proper.

Practice questions

1 Limited liability.
2 Shares are owned by friends and family of the original owner; shareholders are likely to share all of the business objectives.
3 If the business goes bust, the Greens will lose only the amount they own in shares.

4 They want to keep close control over the business; if they went plc, anyone could buy shares and influence the decisions of the company.

Pages 14/15

Q Owners of a co-op have only one vote at AGMs no matter how many shares they own. Decisions are taken for the benefit of all members, not just the controlling shareholder group.

Q The franchiser name would be well known and the franchisee also benefits from the larger firm's marketing.

Practice questions

1 Mike and Alan would benefit from the larger firm's name and marketing, as well as their trading expertise. They might also get help with the costs of renting a larger store.
2 The franchiser will expect an annual fee or even a share of any profits which they earn. They might also have to trade in a particular way demanded by the franchiser. They 'lose control' of parts of the business.

Pages 16/17

Q They are essential for business transport; a natural monopoly is best in government hands.

Q Private shareholders could expect annual dividends; workers may lose their jobs as part of a cost-cutting exercise, but those in work might be better paid; customers might get better products and services as a result of competition, although prices might also rise, especially in remote areas.

Q For: could introduce new trains more quickly; reduces need for tax payer's money.
Against: some unprofitable services might be cut; profits would go shareholders rather than to benefit the Tube.

Q Schools are provided by both sectors; private suppliers provide goods and services for state schools.

Practice questions

1 Privatisation means the selling of public sector organisations to the private sector.
2 a) The business might now be run more for profit and the interests of shareholders, rather than the interests of the customers and the community.
   b) The quality of products might improve if the private firm decided to put more money into research and development. The quality might get worse if competition led to businesses cutting corners or only running profitable parts of the business.
   c) Privatisation can lead to more competition if other businesses decide to enter the market; prices might then go down. If the business stays

in one private company's hands, prices might rise as there is no control over a monopoly business.

Pages 18/19

Q A manager of a large company would probably have a set of section managers and supervisors who would keep him/her informed. There may also be formal reports made about progress.

Q A school organisation chart would be hierarchical, probably with two sections:

Headteacher

Deputy (curriculum) — Deputy (pastoral)

Heads of department — Heads of year

Staff in each department — Form tutors in each year group

The Head of English will control all teachers of English across the school. The Head of Year 9 will control the tutors who work with Year 9 classes.

Practice questions

1

Jack Davis (chairman)

Irene Davis (managing director)

Paul Singh (finance manager) — Daniel Davis (retail manager) — Chris Davis (production manager)

2 Division of labour means each employee specialising on one part of the production process.

3 Human resource management, distribution, research and development.

4 Chain of command means the line of responsibility for decisions; span of control refers to the range of responsibility for any one person or department.

5 Accounts manager, payroll supervisor.

6 Advantages: clear line of responsibility; opportunities for promotion.
Disadvantages: decisions can take time to pass on; hard for people at the top and bottom to know what the other is doing.

Pages 20/21

Q A statement summarising the main aims of the business.

Q Examples could be: increase profit by 5%, expand sales of a new line, open two stores in new areas, expand sales of mail order by 5% or increase donations to charities by 1%.

Q Both charity shop and grocer would aim for a larger share of their particular 'markets', and to survive long term in their 'business activities'. Both would want to operate efficiently with minimum costs. The grocer would place greater emphasis on profits while the charity shop would want to cover costs. The grocer's

main objective is to supply goods which offer value for money, while the charity shop aims to provide a service to customers in order to help others.

Q Shareholders, managers, employees, customers.

Practice questions

1 It will help the firm to grow, spread risks of trading in the north and could boost their own success.

2 Shareholders' main interest is their reward for investment, the dividend payout which is their share of profits.

3 Customers in the south will have a new choice of products; customers in the north might not get as good a service if the business spends more attention on the launch in the south.

4 Managers might say that everyone's interest is in profit and that, in the years ahead, more profit might be earned from the expansion, even if the dividends are low to start with.

Business production

Pages 22/23

Q A product-led business makes products and then tries to sell them; a customer-led business researches customer needs and makes products to suit.

Q A car company can spread its risks by having a range of different models. If customer tastes for certain models change, then the car company won't lose all its business.

Q Small specialist bakers offer particular products which customers will buy because of their quality. There are many different kinds of customers and some will prefer a small shop to a supermarket.

Practice questions

1 Products popular with customers are given more shelf space. Customer surveys are used to check on quality of service.

2 Supermarkets can use large warehouses to supply their own stores (technical economies). Products can be bought in large quantities straight from the supplier (trading economies). Specialist managers can be employed (managerial economies). Money can be borrowed at competitive rates (financial economies).

Pages 24/25

Q Batch production because the supermarket will want large quantities but covering a range of different cakes to suit different tastes. Machinery can be used while still offering some variety.

Q JIT will cut the storage space needed for furniture parts and thereby save money. Different specialist suppliers can be used to bring in parts just when they are needed and ensure quality. There would, though, be a risk of holding up the work on all items of furniture if a supplier doesn't deliver on time and to the right quality.

Q Team work can speed up the process, improve quality and improve job satisfaction.

Practice questions

1 Batch production is using flow production techniques to make different batches of a similar kind of product. When one batch is finished, production switches to a second style.

2 A clothing manufacturer wants to make basic styles so machinery would cut costs. Different styles, finishes and fabrics may be used in batches so that different kinds of customers can be targeted while still using one factory. Workers with basic skills in cutting fabric can be used and they stay motivated because they have different styles to work on.

Pages 26/27

Q A school's efficiency could be 'measured' by comparing the number of pupils with successful qualifications against the amount spent per pupil. Qualitative measures might also be used, for example, how happy the pupils are, or how much the school buildings are being used.

Q CAM means using computers to aid part of the production process; CIM means using computers to manage the whole process.

Practice questions

1 a) Automation means a production process entirely managed by machinery.
   b) CAM is when computers aid the production process but workers are still involved.
   c) Computer control systems use technology to manage part of the production process, in particular, to turn other machines on and off or to keep track of where items are on a production line.

2 Computers could be used to regulate temperatures or to open windows automatically, to control watering systems and to keep track of the different plants stocked in the hothouses.

3 Capital-intensive businesses have a greater part of their production run by machines than people. More money is invested in machinery than is spent on people's wages.

4 Beau employees might find that new technology could save time and effort if lots of small chores could be done automatically. Workers could then spend more time on the more interesting activities. They might have to be retrained, both to manage the technology and in new jobs. There is also a risk that fewer workers will be needed and some might be made redundant.

Pages 28/29

Q A designer sweatshirt should be well-made, have a good colour which doesn't fade and not shrink in the wash. The item should be exchanged without fuss if it fails to meet these standards in the first six months of wear.

Q In a traditional factory, there would be quality control specialists who would sample products at different stages of production to check on the quality. They might check on the quality of seams sewn by different people, on the quality of colour dyes and make sure that the fabric has no flaws in it.

Q Kaizen is a way of improving quality of production by giving all workers responsibility for quality throughout the process.

Practice questions

1 This could save GRC money by putting the packaging closer to the products. There would be less movement and a manager could keep an eye on the whole process. They could sell the spare site and probably save on some labour costs.

2 a) Quality control means checking the quality of the product and the production process to ensure standards are maintained.
   b) A high standard of quality control could be obtained by employing inspectors to check the kitchen products at different stages in the production process and ensuring that the best quality materials are used. They could also spend time training staff to the highest level of skills. Alternatively, they could train all workers to operate as teams to check on quality throughout the process. Many eyes are more likely to spot problems before they become too serious.

Pages 30/31

Q A large frozen food factory will need to send small sized products out to supermarket wholesale depots. They would be better placed near the suppliers of fish because these are large items and there would be cost savings if these supplies travel only short distances. The power for freezing can come anywhere in the country so the other factors might be the nearby road links and whether workers can be found. It is unlikely that highly-skilled workers would be needed for such a factory, but the firm may require quite large numbers, and so should locate near to a large town or city.

Q A government may encourage a business to move to a particular area through grants; it could discourage a business by planning controls forbidding development, and it could encourage the development of an area generally by supporting modern industrial buildings.

Practice questions

1 Climate; close proximity to a large number of customers; other nearby leisure facilities.

2 Climate first because many activities in an outdoor theme park require good weather to be safe and to be enjoyable. The number of customers comes next; if there are enough, it doesn't matter if there are rival attractions. Rival attractions will bring in customers to the area; they may then use the theme park.

Business finance

Pages 32/33

Q Your regular sources of income are likely to be pocket money and income from part-time work. Your expenditure may include snacks, cinema, CDs (weekly), occasional clothes (monthly) and presents. You may keep a note of your spending, or perhaps get a print-out from a bank savings account. Business finances are different because of the larger number of payments, the range of different cost items, and the need to keep track of payments for the benefit of different stakeholders.

Q Owner's own money, bank loans, government grants.

Practice questions

1 Internal: retained profit, owners' capital, share sales. External: bank loan, lease arrangements, grants.

2 Restaurant owners may not have enough income to pay for a new restaurant. They may need to use their own cash for other purposes.

Pages 34/35

Q Start-up costs: bread-slicer, computer, cleaning equipment, delivery van, staff training.
Running costs: sandwich fillings, electricity, bread, rent, wages.
Renewal costs: repairs to van, replacement equipment.

Q They give a clear picture of how future business activities are going to be managed and financed.

Practice questions

1 You would expect to see details of how they've costed the equipment and their own costs, how they've forecast sales revenue and break even, and how much of the loan they plan to repay each year. You would also require clear agreement about how much interest and repayment will take place each year, the finishing date for repayments and guarantees for the money if the business has difficulties.

2 a) Possibly issue shares or take out a long-term bank loan.

   b) A bank loan, retained profits or possibly lease finance.

   c) Lease it so it could be returned if the business was in difficulty or needed a bigger building.

Pages 36/37

Q Fixed costs: cost of the buses, maintenance equipment, garage.
Variable costs: drivers' wages, tickets, fuel for buses.

Q Break-even level of sales = fixed costs / contribution = 2000/10-8 = 1000.

Q The gaps between the TR and TC lines show losses (to the left) and profits (to the right).

Practice questions

1 Fixed cost: sandwich-making equipment; Variable cost: bread.

2 Break even is when revenue just covers costs; 1000/2-1 = 1000 sandwiches.

3 a) Break-even point = 1000/1.50-1 = 2000 sandwiches. The break-even level doubles.

   b) Break-even point = 1000/2-0.60 = 1000/1.4 = 715 sandwiches. The break-even level falls.

   c) Break-even point = 1200/2-1 = 1200 sandwiches. The break-even level rises.

Pages 38/39

Q The manufacturer will still bear the costs of making the decorations but no income will be coming into the business until the Christmas months.

Q Net cash flow from January to April is worsening as more money is flowing out that in. From May, costs must be cut or sales revenue increased if the business is to be successful.

Practice questions

1 It shows likely flows of income and expenditure for the year ahead.

2 Actual cash flow may show variations in the amount of both income and expenditure. It is likely that the net cash flow will be different from the forecast.

3 Fuzz might be short of cash at certain times of the year, especially prior to Christmas.

4 Fuzz might take a short-term loan in the months before Christmas, or they might try to cut costs.

Pages 40/41

Q It uses a specialist finance department to do the job and regularly draws up financial accounts.

Q Managers of the business wish to know the current state of finances; shareholders of a company would be interested because it gives them an idea of the likely profit to be shared and the security of the company's future; the government will be interested because they wish to calculate the tax due; employees wish to see if the firm is profitable and will still be employing them in the months ahead.

Q Net current assets (in this case £1 400 00).

Practice questions

1 Could look at the working capital (current assets - liabilities) to see how much funding is available for debt repayment.

2 Expansion plans should be based on a healthy cash flow, a decent and regular profit, a healthy amount of retained profit, and a low interest rate if they intend to borrow money.

Pages 42/43

Q They provide detailed information about financial performance.

Q Managers (How well are we doing?) and creditors (Will we get repaid and when?).

Practice questions

1 Current ratio = current assets : current liabilities = 4000:800 = 5:1.

2 The company has a healthy asset position and could afford to use some of these assets to expand the business.

People in business

Pages 44/45

Q HR managers in a large school would supervise relationships between managers, teaching and non-teaching staff, and organise recruitment and training of new and replacement teachers.

Q In the short term, you could offer your workers bonuses for good work, training to help them gain future promotion, and a greater say in decisions so that they feel more involved. In the longer term, a new pay structure which rewarded the best trained and fastest working staff could be introduced. New machinery could be used to replace dreary tasks and you could involve workers in quality management.

Practice questions

1 Workers are poorly motivated because they are not well paid and do not enjoy their jobs.

2 Raise basic pay because it would give them more encouragement to stay on and work hard. Give some additional training - this would give more purpose and responsibility to workers.

Pages 46/47

Q Initially, decent pay and working conditions, and lots of praise from supervisors and managers. Opportunity for training and promotion, and involvement in decisions may then become more important to provide more job satisfaction.

Q Overtime is paid for working beyond normal hours and is often paid at a higher rate. Bonuses are paid for a specific job, often to urgent deadlines.

Practice questions

a) Cleaner: payment by results and a good basic wage because the job is very satisfying.

b) Salesperson: commission so it encourages him or her to work faster or push a deal more effectively.

c) Nurse: basic salary because results are hard to quantify.

d) Shop assistant: time rate with bonuses because the job is relatively unskilled and you want the worker to make good use of time.

e) Lorry driver: basic wage with opportunity for overtime. You don't want a system which encourages the driver to work flat out because this could be dangerous, but probably need overtime because the time to complete a job can be unpredictable.

Pages 48/49

Q Draw up a job and person specification, advertise locally and then have a short interview with a practical demonstration to assess the candidates' skills. Alternatively, the manager might use the recommendation of a fellow café manager and talk to someone directly without the need for adverts.

Q A job description lists all the duties of a particular job; a person specification identifies the characteristics of the ideal employee for a job.

Practice question

The job description gives a clear vision of the job expectations and can be used later to check the progress of the appointed person. Interviews give both interviewer and candidate an opportunity to meet and decide if they'll get on successfully. This is particularly important in terms of a small business where people have to work closely together with a lot of trust.

Pages 50/51

Practice questions

1 Karen because she offers better GCSE grades, some post-16 study, has a reliable, if limited, work experience and an interest in computers.

2 What are your strengths? And areas for development? How well do you get on with people? What do you know about computers? Why are you applying for this post? What training do you think you will need? Where do you see yourself in five years time? (These questions will find out about attitude, experience, self-awareness and ambition.)

3 Internal recruitment means finding someone from within the current employees. This can save a lot of time and money, you know the strengths of the person and they know your business.

Pages 52/53

Q The supermarket will get more reliable staff who shouldn't make as many mistakes; the employees will gain new skills which might help them to win promotion within the firm or outside.

Q Karen will want to know what is expected of her, how machines work, any time and behaviour rules, who she is going to work with and where she is going to work, who she sees with any problems, and where the 'domestic' places are, for example, canteen and toilets.

Q The first takes place at the employee's usual workplace; the second is provided by a trainer at a different site.

Q Local IT training may be financed by government but run by businesses. Modern apprenticeship training is funded by government and provided by local colleges and firms. In both cases, firms may have to contribute but they get a re-skilled worker and part of the costs are covered by the government. Employees get opportunities which would otherwise pass them by.

Practice questions

The company might not have the expertise or the

spare managers/supervisors to do the training internally. Outside trainers may be more up to date.

Pages 54/55

Q The travel agent probably didn't double-check the ticket - a system which makes sure both customer and seller have signed agreements might help. There is a lack of guidance in filling out the form - better guidance and a 'cooling-off' period between the order arriving and the customer being billed might help. There is poor communication between the manager and supervisor - agreement over who does the training and who is the new recruit's clear line manager might help.

Q a) Memo: to remind a fellow manager of a simple task which needs doing. b) Formal report: a review of staffing needs in a particular department before reorganisation. c) Personal meeting: a discipline review of a worker with a poor record.

Q Records are kept more efficiently by computers, e-mail allows information to be easily shared inside and outside the company, marketing can be done worldwide via the Internet at low cost.

Practice questions

a) Employer: advantages - saves office costs, employees are better motivated; disadvantages - lose face-to-face contact, not such close supervision.

b) Employee: advantages - can mix home and work life better, added flexibility, cuts travel costs and time; disadvantages - work may be intrusive at home, may incur extra costs (e.g. a printer), can lose personal contact and motivation.

Pages 56/57

Q Good at talking to people; makes employees feel valued; carefully discusses important points; ready to compromise at times.

Q Support in times of trouble; extra quality information; contacts with similar firms.

Q Provides health and safety regulations to make sure workplaces are fit; makes sure that there are equal opportunities for men and women and that there is no discrimination; provides guidelines on minimum wages for the low paid.

Practice question

The employer is breaking the law by not providing written contracts and not following health and saftey guidelines. A trade union could negotiate with employers to change the rules, threaten industrial action if the employer won't change and provide information and guidance for workers in making their case.

Pages 58/59

Q A single union will cut the negotiating time, ensure that all workers are covered by any agreement and make information-sharing easier.

Q There may be agreement about some machines being introduced and some workers getting a pay rise and training. To reach agreement, the employers may have to compromise on how quickly machines are introduced; the skilled workers may have to compromise on relative pay differentials between them and other workers; unskilled workers may have to compromise on the fact that some workers will have to use the new machines.

Q Strikes, overtime ban, work to rule.

Practice questions

1 a) Some orders will be late, but wage costs will be lower.

b) Most production will slow down and some jobs will not get done at all.

c) Orders may be lost, possibly for good if the strike is a long one, but it will save on running costs while the factory is shut.

2 It covers everyone so only one set of negotiations will be needed; there will be no divisions between workers; lines of responsibility will be clearer. If workers need to take action, they will be a more powerful group.

Business and marketing

Pages 60/61

Q Customers could be classified by age group, which facilities they are most likely to use, geographical area or income levels.

Q SWOT analysis provides a clear framework to identify strengths and weaknesses, and any opportunities or threats from the external environment.

Practice question

The company could carry out a SWOT analysis. Strengths: which products are the most profitable, which are growing, customer base? Weaknesses: are there any areas where costs are too high or where marketing is poor, do some product lines need to be closed? Opportunities: could the product be sold more easily across Eastern Europe or China, could the firm introduce new products with, say, colour-matched accessories or better text-messaging? Threats: what is the state of potential markets, is there a global slump, what are rival companies doing, how do their prices and product range compare?

Pages 62/63

Q Market segments are the different groups into which a particular market can be divided for selling purposes. For example, the market for spectacles could be divided into young people, fashion-conscious people of working age, the elderly, etc.

Q Primary data is fresh, collected by researchers, but expensive; secondary data has already been collected and published, is quickly available, is often free, but can be dated.

Q Street surveys, telephone surveys, postal surveys.

Practice questions

1   Typical spending at garages over a period; why they choose a particular petrol station.

2   It would allow the manager to plan a targeted marketing campaign to attract particular kinds of motorist.

Pages 64/65

Q   Price: low compared to shops. Place: direct selling cuts down distribution costs. Promotion: high cost national coverage on TV, aiming for big volume sales of familiar product. Product: packaging should be nothing fancy, TV does the selling, just needs to be safely delivered.

Q   Create a new feature like cold-water wash, improve the performance of the washing powder, target new customers.

Practice questions

1   Large posters for a short period prior to opening, and local leaflets and local newspaper adverts repeated weekly for four weeks prior to opening. This will raise the profile locally and make people aware of the opening. (Costs: five poster sites = £2000; four leaflet sets = £700; four newspaper adverts = £2200.)

2   Once the store is open, sustain new interest via young people with competitions at school (prizes £500), meal discounts (1000 at £2 each = £2000), eight radio adverts (twice daily for four days = £2400). Young people can typically be expected to bring along their families. Once eating habits are established, regular 'give-aways' linked to local cinema programmes could be used to sustain interest.

Pages 66/67

Q   One has a short cycle (computer games) and the other long (salt).

Q   The life cycle of a mobile phone could be extended by adding extra features, linking to the Internet in trendy ways, by offering special text messaging services or links to other fashion accessories.

Q   It helps customers to identify the product, keeps their loyalty, and is good in competition against rivals.

Practice questions

1   A very competitive market is one where lots of rival companies and products are competing for customers. Young people may be able to buy several different shoes with fashionable brands supplied by companies from all over the world. There may be several shoes with very similar prices.

2   Customers may be resistant to a new brand which has no 'street cred'. Allsports may have to spend a large amount of money marketing its brand, for example, having a well-known sports star to champion its product.

Pages 68/69

Q   Axes: price/costs on the vertical, number of tickets on the horizontal. Demand curve slopes down left to right, supply curve slopes up left to right. Draw a horizontal line from the price axis at £20 (above the equilibrium price). At this price it is clear that the volume of tickets supplied is far greater than the volume demanded.

A price of around £15 might fill the hall. This is only an estimate as there is not enough information to draw the exact graphs.

Q   Competitive pricing means matching price to rivals: skimming means setting the highest possible price while the product is special or fashionable.

Practice questions

1   Customers might not try the product at all, or if they do, they will not stay with the product unless the distinctive quality is very good.

2   The company might try a loss-leader pricing policy, setting a very low price for another one of their products in order to catch the customers' eyes. Alternatively, they might try price discrimination by selling their product somewhere special, like in train buffets or in airports.

Pages 70/71

Q   Promotion involves spending on a product so that customers find out about its particular strengths and are persuaded to buy it. Recent examples include Kit Kat's launch of a new orange version of the well known chocolate bar via television advertisements; the government's attempts to attract new teachers by advertising in the cinema and on television, selling teaching as a job of many parts; car firms promoting new products via television with eye-catching adverts featuring cars rushing through flames or being specially designed for women-appeal.

Q   Prime-time TV advertising catches a very large audience, but is very expensive and not all the audience will see the product as being to their taste.

Q   Short-term: one-off direct mailing to local customers. Long-term: a public relations campaign over a year to present a company in a new way.

Practice question

Local adverts will attract local custom and that may well be the best source of new customers for Fill-up Foods plc. It is relatively cheap compared with national advertising but will only reach a limited audience. Local adverts can also be targeted at specific homes via leaflet drops or direct calls on the telephone. The product might be linked into popular local firms.

The business environment
Pages 72/73

Q   Pressure groups may carry out protests at the company's premises which create bad publicity; consumers may boycott their product, resulting in profits falling; governments may fine the company.

Q Sudden rise in interest rates, new invention by rival company, slump in the general economy.

Practice question

The government could help business activity by providing grants for firms that locate in particular places, by cutting taxes for companies, by promoting exports or putting taxes on foreign imports.

Pages 74/75

Q A new restaurant may bring new custom for both, particularly if they are selling a different kind of food. The quality of the existing restaurant might look very good beside a new one.

Q To stop businesses making false claims or advertising undesirable products.

Q Consumers can be protected by laws, voluntary business codes and Trading Standards Officers.

Practice questions

1 The T-shirt was sold as being fit-for-purpose with faded colour. Unless there is some other fault, the customer is not entitled to her money back (Sale and Supply of Goods Act).

2 Baz could encourage the goodwill of the customer by offering another product in exchange.

3 The customer could get advice from the Citizen's Advice Bureau or the local Trading Standards Office.

4 They could take Baz to the small claims court.

Pages 76/77

Q The support and interest of the local community who need to view the business as being good for the community.

Q Potential costs could include pollution during the development, extra traffic and noise once built, ugly appearance and loss of trade for other shops in the community.

Q By charging more for the product; by taxes.

Practice questions

1 External benefits might include extra jobs; more spending by workers and visitors to the park; higher profile in the area as a place to visit; the by-pass might be built as part of the development; there might be contributions to a special art feature donated by the park.

2 External costs might include pollution during the development; extra traffic and noise once built; ugly appearance; loss of trade for other leisure attractions in the area.

3 The local council could charge higher business rates, or ask the park to contribute to some other development. The government could tax such developments or ask them to pay a planning fee of some kind. Alternatively, general taxes could be used to cover some of the community costs.

Pages 78/79

Q Provide stability for businesses; help the poor; provide essential goods and services.

Q The government could spend more on public sector activities to boost spending in the economy. It could also pursue policies which would encourage lower interest rates, or lower taxes in a bid to get consumers to spend more.

Q One is a tax on income, the other a tax on spending.

Practice questions

1 It means Carco will be able to locate at Kirston with cheaper rates and with local grants to help them.

2 Carco will also benefit from the town's new infrastructure and a ready workforce.

3 Their arrival may encourage other businesses to locate in Kirston and their workers will spend money in the local community. Carco may also purchase products from local businesses. They will eventually pay business rates to the local council.

Pages 80/81

Q Protects the rights of workers and consumers; aid for farmers; easier trade between countries.

Q For: Businesses would find it less complicated to trade. Against: The government would lose some control over the economy.

Practice questions

1 A single market is a shared trading area with common external barriers to protect members and free trading between members within the boundaries.

2 This helps because there are no taxes between the member countries, a common currency makes trade easier and there are common rules about advertising, transport, etc.

3 Firms which set up factories in the EU get grants to help them if they bring employment and are allowed to trade within the EU because their products are made inside the EU boundaries.

Pages 82/83

Q Global competition means rival businesses competing across the world.

Q Any firm exporting to the US will now find that their products cost less for Americans to buy, because US dollars now buy more British products.

Q Tariffs, quotas, subsidies to UK firms.

Practice questions

1 a) Japanese visitors will find their yen buys more British pounds. This could encourage more Japanese visitors to come to the craft centre as part of a foreign holiday.

   b) Japanese consumers will have less money to spend and may cut back on foreign holidays. This is likely to mean that fewer visitors come to the craft centre.

2 The government could help to keep the exchange rate stable so that Jo's business is not disrupted by unexpected fluctuations. It could also pursue policies which promote lower interest rates so that Jo can expand her business through cheaper loans.

Business types & objectives (page 100)

1

Business sector	Kind of business activity
Primary	*Extracting raw materials*
Secondary	Using raw materials to produce finished goods
Tertiary	*Providing a service*

2 a) Oil extraction

b) Oil refining to produce plastic

c) Toy manufacturing using plastic

d) Toys to wholesaler

e) Toys to retailers

f) Consumer buys toys

3

	Sole trader	Partnership
Decision making	Sole responsibility	*Shared responsibility*
Profits	*All go to owner*	Shared between partners
Start-up finance	Needs to find all the finance	*Shared responsibility for raising finance*
Liability	Unlimited	*Unlimited*

4

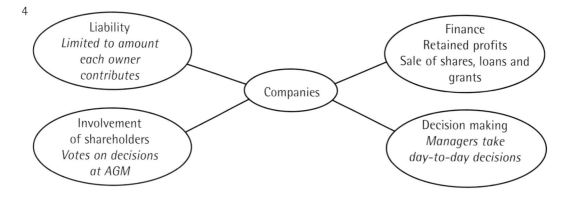

5

	Benefits for hotel company (franchiser)	Benefits for local manager (franchisee)
Start-up	Business grows without large debts.	Less problems during start-up.
Profits	*Often receives a share of profits.*	Keeps most of profits (% might go to franchiser).
Management	Only central management needed. Less hassle than opening new branch.	*Local manager knows local needs. Operates like 'own boss'.*
Training and quality	Provide central training, but get people with local knowledge. Ensure quality standards.	*Training provided.*

6

7

Suppliers	Repeat orders and reliable payment
Local community	Local jobs and clean environment
Employees	Good pay, job satisfaction and security
Shareholders	Good return on investment
Customers	Value for money
Managers	Good salary, status and successful department

Business production (page 102)

8

Product choice	Examples	Advantages	Disadvantages
Business with sole product	Toy firm just making balls	Good if product in great demand	*Risky if market falls*
Business with wide product range	*Company making different toys*	*Spreads risk across a range of products*	Difficult to manage Can raise costs
Business with wide product mix	Unilever: makes food and cleaning products, etc.	*Spreads risk across a range of products and markets*	*Difficult to manage Can raise costs*

9

Technical	Using machinery more efficiently (five small firms, five fork lift drivers: one large firm, three fork lift drivers)
Trading	Buying materials in bulk so unit cost falls
Financial	Borrowing larger sums of money at lower rates of interest
Managerial	Large firm able to hire specialist managers

10

Examples	Advantages	Disadvantages
Job production *House extension*	High quality product made by skilled workers Job satisfaction high Easy to isolate problem areas	*High unit cost Slow production Needs highly skilled workers*
Batch production *Sofa manufacturing*	*Lower costs through use of machinery Provide a range of products Flexible to market changes*	Costly storage needed Some repetition in jobs Batches need to be moved Machinery needs resetting
Flow production *Family cars*	Large output, low unit cost *Less training for unskilled workers Make good use of CIM Can meet orders quickly*	Large investment in machinery Inflexible assembly line Repetitive work, poor motivation Products all the same Breakdowns cause big problems

11 Engine assembly   Bodywork shaping   Wheel and seats   Body fitted to chassis   Final parts added
                              and spraying   on chassis

engine blocks   metal for car body   tyres   windscreen
                       paint for car body   wheel suspension   headlights
                                                     seat covers

12 **Business managers**
    A product which is better than other firms' products
    A product with quality but that doesn't cost too much to make
    A product where machinery can be used to ensure quality

    Customers
    A product which lasts a long time
    A product with distinctive looks
    A product with a well-known brand name

    Government
    A product which passes safety checks
    A product which meets or exceeds industry standards
    A product which is environmentally friendly in production

13 a) Labour: *may need specialist labour, lots of workers, workers very close by*
    b) Raw materials and the market: *may need to be near heavy raw materials (e.g. steel), or near market for delivery (e.g. heavy machinery, houses)*
    c) Climate: *may need good weather for outdoor activities, or good growing conditions*
    d) Cost of land: *high costs in city centres, low costs if a long way from development*
    e) Roads: *may need good access to a range of cities or to Europe, big lorries may need access*
    f) Government grants: *some areas have grants for employment, for development or for avoiding some areas*

Business finance (page 104)

14

Source	Features	Used for
Internal		
Retained profits	Money earned. No interest to pay, easily available. Most common source of finance.	Running costs first. Also, potentially, renewal and expansion.
Investments	Money put in by owners or, if a limited company, obtained by selling shares. Usually long-term commitment.	*Start-up, buying equipment, expansion.*
Lease of assets	A 'one-off' for raising money, generally when a business is struggling.	*Equipment, emergency costs.*

Source	Features	Used for
External		
Overdrafts	Money can be withdrawn, even if little in the bank already. Short-term agreements, high interest charged.	Covering gaps in cash flow.
Loans	Money from banks or other sources. Arranged to cover different time periods, with different interest rates. Often need guarantees to ensure pay-back.	*Start-up, equipment.*
Grants	Money from government, generally tied in to fixed commitments such as improving a region's unemployment or environment.	*Start-up, equipment.*
Trade credit	Buying goods, but not paying for them until an agreed later date.	*Buying stock.*
Hire purchase	Payments are spread over time, so less money committed in the short term. Interest is charged, but item (e.g. equipment) eventually owned outright.	Buying equipment, renewal.

15 *Section 1: Introduction, the business and partners: executive summary (key points)*
Section 2: The new product and its possible sales in the market
Section 3: Production costs and break even estimates
Section 4: Projected cash flow
Section 5: Loans required and repayment schedule
Section 6: Contingency plans

16 a) The break-even point shows *when costs are just covered by revenue.*
b) The business will make a profit when *revenue is above costs.*
c) Profit is shown in the graph by the area *between the TR and TC curves to the right of the break-even point.*
d) At the current production level the business will make a loss because *the output level is below that needed for break even.*
e) The business could become more profitable if it *increased output, or reduced costs or raised the price.*

17a)

	January	February	March	April
Cash in	10 000	10 000	4000	3000
minus				
Cash out	8500	6500	5000	5000
=				
Net cash flow	1500	3500	-1000	-2000
plus				
Opening balance	2500	4000	7500	6500
=				
Closing balance	4000	7500	6500	4500

17b)   *Overall, cash flow for January to April is in a healthy position.*

17c)   If the business is to be successful in the months ahead, the following must happen to net cash flow during May to December: *either cash outflow must fall or cash inflow increase so that net cash flow is positive.*

18

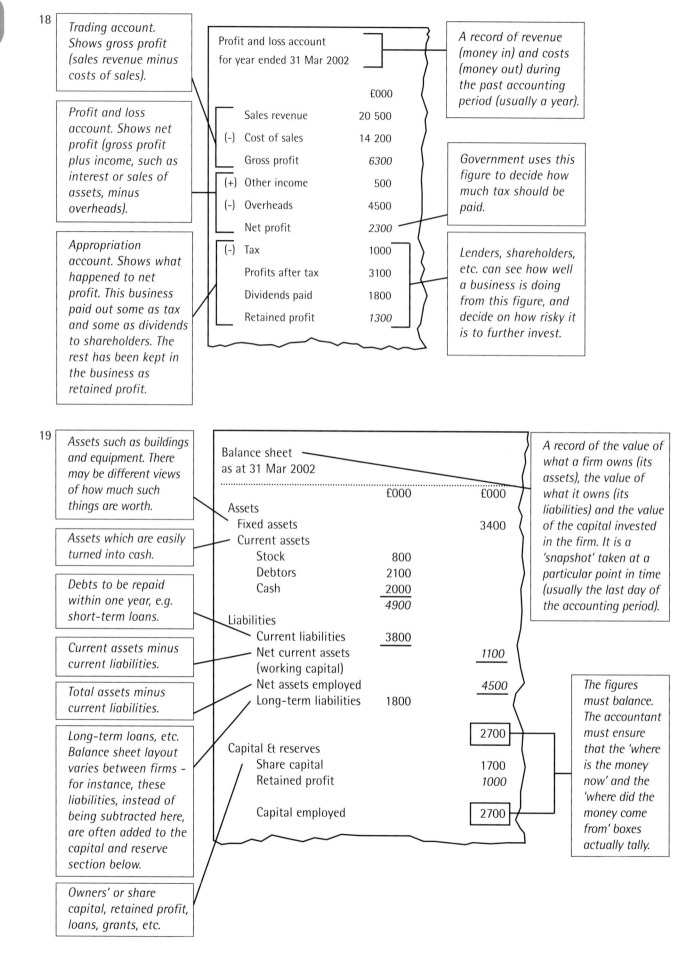

Trading account. Shows gross profit (sales revenue minus costs of sales).

Profit and loss account. Shows net profit (gross profit plus income, such as interest or sales of assets, minus overheads).

Appropriation account. Shows what happened to net profit. This business paid out some as tax and some as dividends to shareholders. The rest has been kept in the business as retained profit.

Profit and loss account
for year ended 31 Mar 2002

		£000
	Sales revenue	20 500
(-)	Cost of sales	14 200
	Gross profit	*6300*
(+)	Other income	500
(-)	Overheads	4500
	Net profit	*2300*
(-)	Tax	1000
	Profits after tax	3100
	Dividends paid	1800
	Retained profit	*1300*

A record of revenue (money in) and costs (money out) during the past accounting period (usually a year).

Government uses this figure to decide how much tax should be paid.

Lenders, shareholders, etc. can see how well a business is doing from this figure, and decide on how risky it is to further invest.

19

Assets such as buildings and equipment. There may be different views of how much such things are worth.

Assets which are easily turned into cash.

Debts to be repaid within one year, e.g. short-term loans.

Current assets minus current liabilities.

Total assets minus current liabilities.

Long-term loans, etc. Balance sheet layout varies between firms - for instance, these liabilities, instead of being subtracted here, are often added to the capital and reserve section below.

Owners' or share capital, retained profit, loans, grants, etc.

Balance sheet
as at 31 Mar 2002

	£000	£000
Assets		
Fixed assets		3400
Current assets		
Stock	800	
Debtors	2100	
Cash	2000	
	4900	
Liabilities		
Current liabilities	3800	
Net current assets (working capital)		*1100*
Net assets employed		*4500*
Long-term liabilities	1800	
		2700
Capital & reserves		
Share capital		1700
Retained profit		1000
Capital employed		2700

A record of the value of what a firm owns (its assets), the value of what it owns (its liabilities) and the value of the capital invested in the firm. It is a 'snapshot' taken at a particular point in time (usually the last day of the accounting period).

The figures must balance. The accountant must ensure that the 'where is the money now' and the 'where did the money come from' boxes actually tally.

20	Ratio	What does it show?	Who might be interested?
	Gross profit margin 15%	That the gross profit is 15p for every £1 of sales.	Managers because they want to see how the firm is performing. Creditors because they want to see good profits to get loans repaid.
	Current ratio 3:1	A firm has three times the money needed to cover debts. Money could be put to better use.	Managers and creditors will want to know how easily the firm's debts can be covered.
	Acid test ratio 1:1	This matches debts against current assets after stocks are discounted. This is a reasonable figure.	Managers and creditors will want to know how easily the firm's debts can be covered.

People in business (page 107)

21	Idea	This will be good because ...
	Pay 1) good basic wage Pay 2) bonuses linked to targets Pay 3) commission on big sales	Ensures everyone feels looked after Encourages staff to try harder Encourages staff to try to sell ambitious amounts
	Benefit 1) training for every two years of service Benefit 2) three-monthly appraisal Benefit 3) certificates of merit	Keeps staff for long periods Makes staff feel valued Gives status within the company

22 *Step 1 Draw up the job description and the person specification.*
Step 2 Advertise the job.
Step 3 Compare applications to the person specification to arrive at a shortlist for interview.
Step 4 Interview the candidates; select the most suitable person.
Step 5 Check references.
Step 6 Draw up a contract and arrange induction training.
Step 7 Monitor the performance of the new staff member through an appraisal system.

23		Advantages	Disadvantages
	Employer	Ensures good staff Ensures better production Helps to keep staff loyal	Training costs money and time Need to find temporary staff Can mean staff seek better jobs elsewhere
	Employee	Provides extra job satisfaction Opportunity for promotion Makes job transfer possible	May mean pay reduction while training Disruption to normal work Can mean extra study and tests

24	Channel of communication	Task	Reason
	Memo	A manager's reminder to her secretary to rearrange a meeting	Simple message between two people who know each other well
	E-mail	A short instruction about a new product to be sent to 120 sales staff	Reaches everyone in same way quickly; cuts paperwork
	Telephone call	A follow-up to a customer complaint about a product	Personal message; makes customer feel important; helps to ensure accurate information
	Meeting with all staff	Latest information about staff redundancies	Very important topic; makes everyone see the importance; can avoid misunderstanding

25 • A successful business needs *employers* and *workers* who respect each others' rights and a decision-making process which ensures fair play.

• Industrial *relations* is the term used to describe the relationship between the workforce and the management of a business. Good relationships mean that difficult *issues* can be sorted out openly and fairly.

• In any business, issues involving staff and management might be small day-to-day ones like *lateness* or sorting out *job roles*, but there are also important issues like *pay* or the introduction of new working methods, which affect the whole of a workforce.

• Businesses, especially large ones, need good organisation and a clear line of *responsibility* so that everyone knows what to do or who to talk to if problems arise.

• Everyone wants their business to be a success, but employers may be more concerned about cutting *costs* and selling products for *profit*. Workers may be more concerned about *decent pay and job security*. Both groups have to balance the protection of their own interests with their shared concern to produce goods on time for customers.

Business and marketing (page 109)

26 **Primary data (original)**
  * *Up-to-date*
  * *Managed by business*
  * *Can target specific market segments*
  * *Can be expensive*
  * *Can keep it confidential*

Secondary data (published)
  * Wide range of data available
  * *Quick to handle*
  * *Usually free*
  * *Can be dated*
  * *Available to everyone*

27

Product	Place
* Update the product features * Develop new range of products * Change the size and packaging * Improve the quality of the product	* Choose to sell through supermarkets * Change delivery times and stock levels * Improve after-sales service
Promotion	**Price**
* Change the timing of adverts * Advertise in the press; on TV; at point-of-sale * Increase expenditure on advertising * Use posters, adverts and local leafleting	* Use a loss-leader to attract customers * Adjust basic price level * Offer discounts * Have different prices for different customers

28a)

28b) i) *Extra advertising*
   ii) *New packaging*
   iii) *Special deals*
   iv) *Change product image*
   v) *Diversify the product*

29

Policy	Definition
Cost-plus pricing	Add a mark-up to the total cost of each product
Competitive pricing	Set price close to those of competitors
Loss-leader	Set price at or below cost (with no mark-up) in order to penetrate a new market
Skimming (or creaming) the market	Set a high price while the product is fashionable
Price discrimination	Charge different prices to different people for the same product
Consumer-led pricing	Set prices which consumers are happy to pay as reasonable value for money

The business environment (page 110)

30 (Any suitable answers should be accepted.)

External influence	Example
Business rivals taking advantage of new technology to bring out a new product	Dyson's vacuum cleaner outstrips rival Hoover
An industry setting guidelines for all the businesses in that sector	Holiday travel firms providing guaranteed standards against ABTA industry guidelines
Customers' tastes changing	Fashion clothes, food at restaurants
Government introduces a new law affecting business	Nappies not allowed to contain harmful bleaches
Pressure group campaigns against business because of environmental damage	Petrol companies' sales hit by campaigns against their pollution in Nigeria
A slump in another country affects UK business	US crisis after Sept 11th cuts tourists to UK

31

Trading Standards Officers	Check on faulty products, and weights and measures.
British Standards Institute	Tests products for safety and quality. It issues 'Kitemarks' to show that a product has met certain standards.
Office of Fair Trading	Provides information and advice leaflets.
Environmental Health Officers	Check on such things as food hygiene, pollution and illegal waste disposal.
ABTA	Promises to get customers home from holiday if a firm goes bust.
UK Government	Passes laws protecting the consumer.
Citizens' Advice Bureaux	Provide free advice and help people to make complaints.

32
- The activities of a business may be affected by government policies and by the state of the national economy in general. Businesses expect governments to steer the economy towards steady *growth* and to avoid big changes in *prices*, interest rates and exchange rates.
- In the UK, we expect our government to make sure businesses operate fairly but also to provide some goods and services for *consumers*. We expect the government to ensure the poorest are helped by the better-off through taxes and *benefits*.
- The government tries to smooth out the big ups and downs in the business *cycle*.
- Growth in UK business output averages 2-3% a year but it tends to fluctuate in cycles every four to five years. Growth and employment are helped by high *demand* in the economy. If demand outstrips supply, there can be a general increase in prices (inflation) and business *planning* becomes very difficult. If the government raises taxes, it can reduce demand but at the risk of pushing up unemployment and shaking the *confidence* of businesses.
- Rising prices affect jobs with fewer goods bought by consumers leading to falling *sales* and cut backs on employment. Workers may want more pay to cover higher prices and so there is extra upward pressure on business costs.
- The government can help but it can't control all the factors which make business a *risky* activity.

Glossary

A

Acid test ratio Like current ratio but taking out stocks; a more accurate measure of a business's liquidity.

B

Balance sheet A record of the value of what a firm owns (its assets), the value of what it owes (its liabilities) and the value of the capital invested in the firm. It is a 'snapshot' taken at a particular point in time (usually the last day of the accounting period).

Batch production Larger-scale production of 'batches' of similar items.

Branding Developing a product's name with a distinctive logo, colours and packaging, and registering all this to prevent other companies copying it.

Break even The point at which total revenue equals total costs.

Business cycle The ups and downs in the level of general business activity in the country.

Business objectives Shows what a business is setting out to achieve in broad terms and as more detailed targets.

Business plan Shows the information and figures which predict the future performance of the business.

C

CAD/CAM/CIM Use of computers in production to aid or completely manage the process (Computer-aided design, Computer-aided manufacturing, Computer-integrated manufacturing).

Cash flow forecast A way of trying to predict what money will come in and what money will go out of a business over a fixed period.

Chain of command The links in an organisation between people with different roles and responsibilities who take orders and instructions from above and give them to those below.

Chain of production Businesses which contribute to the complete production process from extraction to final sale.

Collective bargaining Most industries and businesses decide pay and other issues by collective bargaining (negotiating as a group rather than as an individual).

Competitive business environment The environment in which a business has to operate, competing against rival businesses in the market.

Co-operative A business run by a group of people with a shared interest in the business, for the benefit of all involved. Each participant has an equal say.

Cost-plus pricing A business adds a percentage mark-up to the total unit costs (variable and fixed) of producing an item.

Current ratio Shows how easily a firm's short-term debts could be paid from current assets.

Customer-led Business which bases its production on market research and customer views.

CV (curriculum vitae) Written by a job applicant. It lists their qualifications, interests and experience.

D

Deed of Partnership A set of rules to follow if trust between partners breaks down.

Desk research Working with published material.

E

Economies of scale Reductions in unit costs when producing larger quantities.

Efficient production Producing the maximum output at the least possible cost.

Equal opportunities law Law which ensures equal opportunities, especially in employment.

Euro From 2002, the Euro has become the single currency for the majority of EU member countries.

European Union A common trading area for 15 countries with many shared benefits.

Exchange rate The value of the UK pound against other currencies.

External communication Communication between the business and its customers or suppliers.

External costs and benefits Costs and benefits of business activity which fall on the community and are not covered by normal prices.

External finance Finance from outside of a business, e.g. bank loans, grants, trade credit.

F

Field research Collecting and analysing information gained first-hand, via interviews and surveys.

Financial and Non-financial Incentive Monetary and non-monetary rewards to motivate workers.

Fixed costs Costs of production which don't vary with the amount made.

Flow (or mass) production Continuous production of identical items, e.g. newspapers, glass bottles.

Franchise Allows a small trader to use a well-known company's trade name, and allows the well-known company to use the experience of local managers.

G

Gross profit margin A measure of the profitability of a business for every £1 of sales.

H

Horizontal integration Businesses choose to link activities in one sector with another in the same sector.

Human Resource department The department responsible for recruitment, training and industrial relations in a large business.

I

Income tax Tax on income; the more you earn, the more you pay.

Induction training Training given to new employees to teach the basic skills required for the job and to introduce the employee to the business and its expectations.

Industrial action Action taken by workers to try to put pressure on the management to accept their point of view. Such action might involve a strike (all workers stop work), an overtime ban or a work to rule (doing only those specific tasks which are outlined in your contract).

Industrial relations The term used to describe the relationship between the workforce and the management of a business.

Internal communication Communication within an organisation which enables people to do their jobs effectively.

Internal finance Finance from within the business's own resources, e.g. share sales, profits.

J

Job production Making of a unique item from start to finish, e.g. a house extension.

Just-in-time (lean) production An efficient way of producing. Stocks of raw materials, parts and components arrive in just the right quantity just in time to be used in the production process.

L

Limited liability Responsibility for the debts of a business is limited to the amount of shares of each owner.

Loss-leaders A policy which sets prices at or below cost (with no mark-up) in order to penetrate a new market.

M

Market segments Businesses divide customers into different groups, or market segments, according to different characteristics.

Marketing mix Made up of elements of Product, Promotion, Price and Place.

Maslow's Hierarchy A model of human needs based on a pyramid; basic needs of survival are at the bottom.

O

Off-the-job training Specialist training which involves employees stopping their usual work.

On-the-job training Training given whilst employees are working.

Organisation chart Shows how a business is divided up by function, by product or by place.

Glossary

P

Partnerships Businesses owned by the partners (there must be a minimum of two and usually a maximum of twenty partners).

Performance-related pay A type of 'payment by results', where pay is linked to achievement of targets.

Person specification Drawn up by an employer, it gives a picture of the ideal candidate for a job, and is used to help decide on the most suitable person for that job.

Price discrimination Charging different prices to different people for the same product.

Primary data Information collected first hand, via interviews and surveys.

Primary sector Businesses involved in getting raw materials from the land or sea, e.g. farming.

Private limited company (Ltd) Company owned by shareholders who have limited liability. Shares only available to friends and family.

Privatisation The sale of public sector organisations to the private sector by selling shares.

Productivity A measure of the output per person.

Product-led A business which makes goods first and then thinks how to sell them.

Product life cycle Products have a natural life cycle which begins with their development, moves through a period of growth to maturity and ends with a loss of sales.

Profit and Loss Account A record of revenue (money in) and costs (money out) during the past accounting period (usually a year).

Public limited company (plc) Company owned by shareholders who have limited liability. Shares available to the general public.

Public sector organisation Owned and run by the government for the benefit of everyone. Financed by sales of goods and services and also from taxes.

R

Return on capital employed (ROCE) How much profit is made for every £1 invested.

S

Secondary data Data such as published accounts, government reports and data from consumer groups.

Secondary sector Businesses using raw materials to produce finished goods, e.g. a computer manufacturer.

Shareholders People who have bought shares in a company and are therefore part owners.

Skimming (or creaming) the market Charging a high price for a product while it is fashionable.

Sole trader A business owned and controlled by one person.

Span of control The range of responsibility of any manager.

Stakeholders People who have an interest in the success of a business. Their objectives are often different.

SWOT analysis Helps a business to look at its strengths and weaknesses, and the opportunities and threats in the market.

T

Tertiary sector Businesses providing a service to industry or to consumers, e.g. banking.

Total quality management (TQM) A system of quality management which places responsibility for quality on all employees throughout the production process.

Trade Unions and Trade Associations Represent some workers and employers in discussions and disputes.

V

Value Added Tax (VAT) A tax on spending (currently 17.5% on most goods and services).

Variable costs Business costs which are linked to the amount of goods or services produced.

Vertical integration Businesses choose to link activities in one sector with those in another.

W

Working capital Current assets – current liabilities: a measure of a business's ability to meet immediate payments.

Last-minute learner

Business types & objectives

Businesses can be classified by sectors, by type and by their different objectives.

Sectors of business activity
- **Primary** sector (extraction, e.g. farming).
- **Secondary** sector (manufacturing, e.g. car company).
- **Tertiary** sector (services, e.g. banking).

Businesses may integrate (link) their production activities, vertically (across sectors) or horizontally (in same sector).

Different types of business
- **Sole traders**: owned and controlled by one person.
- **Partnerships**: owned by 2-20 partners.
- **Companies**: private limited companies (Ltds) and public limited companies (plcs). The 'limited' refers to limited liability. Shareholders are the owners, have a say in running the company and share in its profits.
- **Co-operatives**: run by people with a shared business interest, to benefit all involved. Each participant has an equal say.
- **Franchises**: allows a trader to use a well-known company's trade name and enables the company to benefit from the experience of local managers.
- **Public sector** organisations: owned and controlled by the government. Financed by taxes as well as by selling goods and services.

Business organisation
In a small business, the owner has responsibility for major decisions and so communications can be direct with everyone involved. Larger businesses need a structure and more formal communication. Decisions can be hard to manage with long chains of command or large spans of control.

A large business my be divided up by:
- **function** (e.g. marketing, finance)
- **product** (e.g. Ford vans and cars)
- **geographical area** (e.g. Ford UK, Ford Spain).

Business objectives
Businesses may aim to make a profit, to provide a service or to be charitable.

Stakeholders' objectives are often different:
- customers: value for money, choice
- owners: survival in business, best return on investment
- managers: best salary, status for department
- local community: local jobs, clean environment
- suppliers: repeat orders, reliable payment of bills
- employees: job satisfaction, good pay.

The business environment

- Competition can be good because:
  - it keeps businesses on their toes
  - it gives consumers a choice of products.
- Competition may be bad if:
  - businesses make exaggerated claims for their products
  - a firm dominates the market, ignoring customer views
  - some undesirable products are made for profit (e.g. cigarettes, alcohol).
- The three main laws protecting the consumer are:
  - Trade Descriptions Act (1968 and 1972): stops businesses giving misleading information.
  - Consumer Credit Act 1974: protection when borrowing or buying on credit.
  - Sale and Supply of Goods Act 1994: products have to be of 'satisfactory quality'.
- The external business environment is full of risks:
  - The ups and downs in the economy can make it hard to sell a new product.
  - An unforeseen problem with a product may be found.
  - Rivals may use technology to make a better product.
  - Interest rates may rise, increasing the cost of loans.
  - Exchange rates may change, making foreign trade more difficult.
- **The government** manages the economy to provide stability for businesses and ensure everyone benefits from business activity:
  - It taxes income, spending and business profits.
  - It uses the money for welfare benefits, services like health and education, and investment in new roads and buildings.
  - It aims to support poorer regions of the country, e.g. grants to encourage businesses to locate within a designated area.
- UK businesses operate in a **European Union** shared by 25 countries with a market of some 370 million people:
  - EU rules help and control business activity.
  - Over 51% of the UK's overseas trade is with other EU countries.
  - The EU is financed by contributions from member states and tariffs on imports from outside the EU.
  - EU membership may continue to expand as further European countries join.
  - The Euro is a common currency used by most EU members but not currently the UK.

Business finance

- Finance is essential to pay for:
  - **start-up costs**
  - regular **running costs**
  - **unexpected events**
  - **investment**.
- The **finance** for a business can come from:
  - inside (**internal finance**) via owners' funds, share sales, retained profits
  - outside the business (**external finance**) through loans, grants, trade credit, leasing.

- Good financial management requires a good **business plan**, estimates of **break-even** (where revenue just covers costs) and charging a **reasonable price** for a product.
- A price must be enough to cover fixed and variable costs as well as making a profit.
- Regular **cash flow forecasts** and budgets predict money in and out over a fixed period. A profitable firm, without enough cash to pay its **creditors**, may have to cease trading.

- **Detailed accounts** help managers to judge the success of business activities:

1 Profit and loss account
- A record of revenue (money in) and costs (money out) during the past accounting period (usually a year).
- Different parts of the account are used by different groups to judge progress.
- The trading account shows gross profit (sales revenue – cost of sales).
- Government uses the net profit figure to decide how much tax should be paid.
- Lenders and shareholders use the dividend figure to judge the business's success and to assess how risky it is to invest further.

2 Balance sheet
- A record of the value of what a firm owns (assets), what it owes (liabilities) and the capital invested in the firm. It is a 'snapshot' taken at a particular point in time (usually last day of the accounting period):
  - Assets = fixed assets + current assets (stock + debtors + cash)
  - Liabilities = short-term liabilities + long term liabilities
  - Working capital = current assets – current liabilities
  - Capital & reserves = share capital + retained profit.
- Accountants ensure that the figure for 'where the money is' (assets – liabilities) is equal to 'where the money came from' (capital & reserves).

3 Performance ratios

Ratio	What does it show?	Who is interested?
Profitability		
Gross profit margin $\dfrac{\text{Gross profit}}{\text{Sales revenue}} \times 100\%$	Gross profit for every £1 of sales. The bigger the %, the greater the profit.	Managers – how is the firm performing? Creditors – will loans be repaid?
Net profit margin $\dfrac{\text{Gross profit}}{\text{Sales revenue}} \times 100\%$	As above, but allowing for fixed costs.	As above.
Return on capital employed (ROCE) $\dfrac{\text{Net profit}}{\text{Capital employed}} \times 100\%$	Profit created from each £1 invested.	Shareholders – is investment providing as good a return as other options?
Liquidity		
Current ratio Current assets : current liabilities	How easily a firm's short-term debts can be paid from current assets. Ratio of 1:1 means a firm is only just covering debts.	Managers, creditors – how easily can the firm's debts be covered?
Acid test ratio Current assets – stock : current liabilities	Removes stocks from the equation to give a more realistic measure. A reasonable figure is between 0.5:1 and 1:1.	As above.

People in business

- **Recruitment** and **training** are organised by:
  - the manager (small business)
  - the Human Resource Department (large business).
- Motivation theories help to explain people's behaviour:
  - **Maslow's** Hierarchy ranks people's needs in order of importance. Basic needs must always be met but, in the long term, workers need to feel fulfilled, possibly by being given responsibilities.
  - **Mayo** believed an employee's attitude was more important than anything else. Increasing a worker's job satisfaction was the best form of motivation.
  - **McGregor's** theory X.Y suggests managers have two views of workers: theory X – just after money, need close supervision; theory Y - enjoy work, can be

trusted and seek job satisfaction. Managers are advised to follow theory Y.

- **Financial incentives** (e.g. good wages, fringe benefits) and **non-financial incentives** (e.g. varied work, praise, promotion) affect people's motivation. Different types of payment include:
  - wages and salaries/overtime
  - bonus payments
  - performance-related pay.

- A typical company **recruitment process** includes: a job description; a job advertisement; interviews with candidates; checking references; providing a contract and training.

- Training is vital to a business's success. **Properly trained** staff:
  - are more productive
  - stay longer with a business
  - are more likely to obtain promotion.

- **Induction training** teaches the skills required for a job and introduces the rules of a business.

- **Government training** improves workers' qualifications and helps unemployed people.

- **Good communication** helps people do their jobs effectively. There are several types of communication:
  - internal: between employees in the business
  - external: between the business and its customers
  - written: provides a permanent record (e.g. memos, e-mails, reports)
  - verbal: quick and direct (meetings, telephone calls, conversations).

Many routine tasks can now be done more quickly and easily using ICT.

- **Good industrial relations** are vital:
  - Trade Unions speak for workers; Trade Associations speak for employers.
  - Most industries and businesses decide pay and other issues by collective bargaining.
  - Industrial action (e.g. strikes, working to rule) is difficult and costly but necessary at times.
  - There are laws covering **working conditions**, including equal opportunities and a safe workplace:

Employers must:	Employers must not:
Provide a written statement on conditions, e.g. pay	Discriminate by race, age, gender or disability
Give equal pay for the same work to men and women	Stop a worker from belonging to a trade union
Give benefits to workers who have stayed two years	Employ children under the age of 13
Follow health and safety laws	Dismiss a worker unfairly

Business and marketing

- **SWOT analysis** (Strengths, Weaknesses, Opportunities, Threats) helps a business to plan for the future.
- Businesses use **research** to help develop marketing strategies.
  - Customers are split into market **segments** by income, education and occupation.
  - Focus groups (based on gender, age, race etc.) can be asked their opinion of a product.
  - **Desk research** is conducted using **secondary data**; **field research** involves collecting **primary data**.

- There are different **types of survey**: one-on-one questionnaires; postal surveys; random surveys; surveys based on quotas.

- **Survey questions** can be either **closed** (easy to analyse, but provides limited data) or open (provides more information, but harder to analyse).

- The **marketing mix**: 'four Ps':
  Product, Promotion, Price and Place.
  - Different companies emphasise different elements of the marketing mix.

1 **Product**: e.g. quality, range, after-sales service, features and facilities, size and packaging.
2 **Price**: e.g. basic price level, discounts, different pricing for different customer segments.
3 **Promotion** (vital at product launch): e.g. how much expenditure, style and substance, timing, media.
4 **Place**: e.g. what distribution chain to use, direct selling, delivery and stock levels.

- Products have a natural **life cycle**: development and launch; growth to maturity; market is full of similar products; loss of sales; end of cycle.

- The **product development** process involves: establishing customer needs; generating new ideas; checking production is possible; testing prototypes; developing a marketing strategy.

- **Product life cycles** can be lengthened by: extra advertising and promotion; new packaging; special deals; widening the product range; changing the product image; diversifying a product.

- **Branding** involves developing a distinctive name and logo, colours and packaging.

- Prices, supply and demand theory:
  - The higher the price: the more will be supplied; the less will be demanded.
  - Too low a price: demand will outstrip supply.
  - Too high a price: there will be a surplus of unsold products.
  - The equilibrium price will satisfy both a business and its customers.
- **Pricing policies** are used to persuade customers to buy a product:
  - cost-plus pricing (a percentage mark-up)
  - competitive pricing (price like competitors')
  - loss-leaders (prices below cost to penetrate a new market)
  - skimming the market (high price while in fashion)
  - price discrimination (charging different prices to different people for the same product).
- Most companies **advertise** through a variety of media: TV, radio and cinema; newspapers and magazines; journals or specialist publications; posters.
- **Sales promotion activities** include: special offers; price discounts; vouchers, coupons and customer loyalty cards; joint promotions; point of sale materials; free gift campaigns or prize competitions.

Business production

- Business production involves the use of **raw materials**, **labour** and **capital/investment** with an entrepreneur to **take the risks**.
- Production can be product-led or customer-led.
- Different businesses may produce a single product, a wide product range or a wide product mix.
- Larger firms can take advantage of **economies of scale** (reductions in unit costs when producing larger quantities). Economies of scale may be:
  - **technical** – using machinery more effectively
  - **trading** – buy in bulk
  - **financial** – borrow more at lower rates of interest
  - **managerial** – use highly-skilled management.
- There are three production methods, each with its own advantages and disadvantages:

	Advantages	Disadvantages
Job production	High quality product Job satisfaction high	Expensive materials and labour Slow process
Batch production	Lower unit costs More specialised machinery	Costly storage and movement Some repetition in jobs Machinery needs resetting
Flow production	Large output, low unit cost Good use of production time Low-skilled, easily-trained labour Products of standard quality	Large investment in machinery Inflexible; breakdowns expensive Boring work

- **Business efficiency** (maximum output at the least possible cost) can be measured by:
  - productivity (e.g. output per person)
  - unit costs (total costs divided by quantity produced)
  - other measures (e.g. stock levels, product quality).
- **Just-in-time** (or lean) production is an efficient way of producing if carefully managed:
  - parts in just the right quantity, just in time to be used, saving time and money
  - computer-controlled information links are vital
  - breakdowns in the system can be costly.
- Use of **computers in business production** can cut labour costs but requires big investment:
  - CAM (computer-aided manufacturing)
  - CAD (computer-aided design)
  - CIM (computer-integrated manufacturing).

There are various methods of **quality control**:

- sample checks by specialists
- research and development departments (develop new products)
- total quality management (responsibility for quality on all employees, e.g. Japanese idea of continual improvement (Kaizen); workers suggest improvements wherever possible).

- **Factors affecting business location**:
  - labour (e.g. need for a highly skilled workforce)
  - raw materials and the market (e.g. be near to where goods are produced or sold)
  - land (e.g. amount and cost of land, planning restrictions)
  - infrastructure and services (e.g. good communications and transport links)
  - UK and European governments' financial support (e.g. tax-free grants and subsidies).